SUBSOCCER

Football from the Bottom Down

by

ROB KING

with cartoons by
ROD MCLEOD

SOUVENIR PRESS

First published 1985 by Souvenir Press Ltd,
43 Great Russell Street, London WCIB 3PA
and simultaneously in Canada

ISBN 0 285 62706 6

Photoset and printed in Great Britain by
Redwood Burn Limited
Trowbridge, Wiltshire

Most of what follows is true.

What isn't, ought to be.

Contents

Introduction

What is Subsoccer?

Of course, you have to begin a book like this with a question like that. But asking it is one thing; answering it is another. If one pauses between swilling down Pernod and puffing at those foul-smelling French cigarettes with the funny names, to mutter 'What is life?' there are whole troops of philosophers (Sartre, Rousseau, Revie, Robson, etc.) ready with their own endorsed definitions. But Subsoccer is different.

Most of the leading thinkers on the game (or subgame) are either in gaol or insane. And this explains, you see, the vital importance of reading this book. So here, to start with, are just a few words on what Subsoccer isn't.

In spite of its name it is not a sort of alternative sport for all those Number Twelves who spend Saturday after Saturday shivering on the touchline, hoping against hope for the tiniest little compound fracture that will, for once, let them have a go. I'm afraid they must shiver on. Still, the idea does bring us a little nearer to the truth. Subsoccer sides never have substitutes (well, hardly ever) and people who waste their time turning up but not quite turning out do tend to sink hopelessly into sublife instead.

Perhaps we can slightly reshape the definition of the traditional difference between proper soccer and rugby and use that as a starting point.

Subsoccer, then, is a game for gentlemen, hooligans and

lunatics, both harmless and dangerous, played by gentlemen, hooligans and lunatics, both dangerous and harmless.

At once the superiority of this great sport over the two other pastimes (of which it can sometimes seem an uneasy blend, I must admit) is strikingly clear. Subsoccer welcomes all would-be players as they are and happily destroys them without a care for class, caste or cheque-book. Equality is the rule. Its critics – and there are many of them, since anyone who doesn't play the game naturally hates it – would say that all subsoccermen enjoy the equality of the damned. In a way, they are right. Every Subsoccer dressing-room should (although none does) have a notice over its door with 'Abandon hope, all ye who enter here' picked out on it in Adidas-style lettering. I'm sure it's only the sad fact that, until fairly recently, most subteams had no dressing-room door at all – possibly as a result of having no dressing-room – that has denied Dante to the masses. As it is, most submen probably believe he's a swarthy, ruthless sweeper with one of the Milan clubs. Inferno, say.

Still, it can be said that in so far as it is played by (more or less) twenty-two players in (more or less) two teams with a (more or less) round ball, Subsoccer is loosely derived from soccer itself. More or less. It is a football variant, but only in the way that gin is a variant of tea. And so, of course, its name. It may have been applied to the game for the first time fairly recently – one page ago, in fact – but it does seem to capture the sense of the sporting underworld in which we suffer. It also catches the relationship between The Real Thing, demonstrated on *Match of the Day* and so on, and Our Own Thing, done to death on a shadowy half-land of mud-patch pitches from Haverfordwest to Halifax, and from Hereford to Hackney.

Law One

*Subsoccer is likely to occur at any time under any given set
of conditions, but just as likely not to.*

None of this implies that Subsoccer is confined to council parks
and other no-go areas. Far from it, since the game knows no
boundaries. It can be a kickabout on the stretch of wasteland
behind the steelworks, but it could also be, for example, the
European Super Cup Winners' Cup Winners' Cup, or whatever,
at Anfield itself.

Oh yes. Or rather, oh no. Floodlight pylons don't frighten off
the Spirit of Subsoccer the way crucifixes discourage vampires.
Subsoccer can strike at any time and in any place, transforming
the real game into a real shambles at a swift and sudden stroke.
Several First Division clubs, not all unsuccessful, have suffered
from it for whole seasons on end; one of them, in fact, reached
Wembley not so long ago. As it was the usual kind of Cup Final,
nobody noticed.

Law One of Subsoccer explains this strange phenomenon very
neatly. Its revelation will no doubt set many arthritic knees
knocking, since a lot of people will be asking themselves, 'Which
game do I play?' There is only one answer. If you even have to
ask the question at all, you are quite definitely a Subsoccer col-
league, like it or not. They say you learn something new every
day, and it can't all be good, can it? But don't despair; just think
of it as a vocation, to which many are called and – unusually –
all are chosen. No selection worries there.

If, on the other hand, you can't quite accept this – and subsoccermen are, almost by definition, dreadfully self-deluding – I
would advise you to turn to the Church. In this I recommend the
acid test advocated by a clerical friend of mine, a truly awful
goalkeeper for a side that deserved him. He was a trainee vicar at
the time, a reverend-in-waiting who would prop up the bar in

the Windmill on Clapham Common and breathe Young's Special and vaguely religious pronouncements on anybody in range. He used to say that through these impromptu and drunken sermons, he made up in souls for what he gave away in goals. Actually, he used to say that quite often. But he did coin one undeniably perceptive phrase that he took to muttering just before Last Orders.

'By their fouls shall ye know them!' he would rumble, seconds before sprinting for the Gents, and I really believe this is as reliable a means as any for picking out the subconscious subsoccerman. As I hope to make clear, the subgame enjoys or suffers – depending on which end of the boot you happen to be at the time – a degree of desperate violence and decadent brutality matched only at the very highest levels of the sport. There is no contradiction here. Extremes do meet, and the true connoisseur is irresistibly reminded, as he watches, say, Manchester United getting a bit physical at Old Trafford, of the Gasworks Social putting it about on Bromley Rec.

Now, more discerning readers may already be wondering why no volume on this great subject of Subsoccer has ever appeared before. Given all those thousands of subsoccermen who have apparently cursed and kicked their way through life, there must have been *somebody* capable of putting pen to paper, so why should I be the first to spill the so-called beans? It's because all the others have fallen into the very trap I have so cunningly avoided. Every subsoccerman could write this book. The fact that none of them have is due to the fatal error they made in postponing their own autobiographies until the end of what they laughingly called their careers.

By then, of course, it is too late. The subgame completes its destruction in those final, fearful years in the seventh team. When wild-eyed wives and children eventually rip the rotting boots from their clutching fingers, the ex-subsoccermen are shunted

'By their fouls shall ye know them!' he would rumble, seconds
before sprinting for the Gents.

off onto management committees. There they witter away and are wittered away at until they succumb to a sort of self-induced communal hypnosis. They come to believe that they're not ex-submen at all, but ex-soccermen; that soccer and Subsoccer are one and the same game; even that there is no such thing as Sub-soccer! When they reach this stage, all hope is gone.

The process is inevitable. I write this account in the first flush of youth – all right, the second or third flush of youth – because I'm still able to write it at all. I write it on the sound subgame principle of getting them before they get you, which the real game calls retaliating first. But I also write it knowing that in ten years' time, even perhaps in ten months' time, I shall simply refuse to accept that I ever wrote it. I shall use complex reasoning to prove that I could never, ever, have played that terrible game, let alone written about it. With luck, expert medical care, and continuing cheques from the publishers, I may be forced to face the awful truth. I hope so. Some write for posterity; I write for my future sanity.

Law Two
There are no laws of Subsoccer, not even this one, and if there are they are not very often applied anyway.

Even this early, then, it must be obvious that Subsoccer really needs to be experienced to be believed, let alone understood, and this engaging little book is meant to offer that experience in a second-hand but certainly safer way. Sadly, some might be fool-ish enough to feel that reading even this far is enough. Now that they've discovered the First Law of Subsoccer, they may imagine they can learn about the game simply by reading up on its rules.

They could find them all in these pages, but that really wouldn't help; because after the first law comes the second.

Law Two of Subsoccer is set out opposite. Anybody who has ever studied the performance of the referee during the average submatch will realise just how true it is.

Here, then, is knowledge for anyone that seeks it, my sole and solitary purpose being to introduce others to the joys of the game that has wrecked my life. Why should I suffer alone? Once you have read this book, several reactions may suggest that you, too, are a potential subsoccerman, ready to spread a little terror of your own. Unless my words have been in vain, you will immediately begin to show healthy signs of the competitive spirit. You will scythe down the cat, taking it just above the knee as it pads towards the fire. You will hideously bodycheck the wife as she brings in the tea. You will send your son for the paper and whip his legs away from behind as he leaves the room.

Finally, in a frenzy of total commitment, you will hurl this book into the air and aim at it a tremendous kick. You will miss. Do not worry. That is what Subsoccer is all about.

1
The Preparation

Law Three
Add half-an-hour to the time agreed for any meeting
before the game, but one hour if there is a decent pub in
the area or a big race on television.

Subsoccer conditions establish themselves long before the first
foot sinks ankle-deep in the penalty-area swamp. They usually
do so the night before the match in the home of the captain, secretary, manager, or whichever mad masochist is responsible for
running the team.

Not that the captain, secretary, manager or mad masochist
will be at home at the time; not if he has any experience of the
subgame. In fact, he will be anywhere in the world *but* at home.
Ideally, he will find a pub he's never been to before (there must
be a couple left), where he can't easily be traced. Failing that, he
will come up with any sort of excuse, however unlikely, for
being out of the house for the next few hours. Improbability is
no problem here. He could, say, be going to a Barry Manilow
concert. Or walking the goldfish. Or even, in desperation,
watching Orient.

Anyway, the important thing is that he gets away. Because
back at home the telephone will start ringing at around six-
thirty, and will continue to ring at one-minute intervals until
long after midnight. When the wanderer returns, he will find his
wife a broken woman, gibbering over the receiver and staring

16

fixedly at dozens of cryptic, contradictory and downright daft messages scrawled all over the scraps of paper that litter the room. A veteran captain, secretary, manager or mad masochist will lead the poor girl away to bed, pausing only to throw all the pathetic little notes into the bin. He knows quite well, you see, that the whole palaver will begin again the next day, when the real business of salvaging something like a side will start in earnest.

Just after dawn he locks himself in with the telephone and spends the morning trying to decipher messages apparently never meant to convey sense or meaning to the human brain. Generally, they reach him second-hand, passed on by some hopeless, helpless middle-man; and they range from the *Times* Crossword-type – 'New inn no good half-way okay ed' – to those packed with monumentally irrelevant information – 'Charlie says the back-four bloke with black hair called Ginger is in trouble about his boots because his half-sister's having quins in Ashby-de-la-Zouche but the Elephant's fine anyway'.

MEETING WITH DISASTER

Once he's made some sort of stab at scraping together eleven men for the afternoon humiliation, the embattled organiser (I use the term loosely) picks out a rendezvous point handy for everyone but himself. By some strange quirk, and in spite of their general convenience, these always seem to be chosen in a way that takes no account of the personal feelings of anyone who accidentally arrives on time. Everyone else is inevitably late, and I know that I've spent whole years of my life hanging around outside public lavatories, waiting for the others. It's very difficult to look normal in these circumstances, especially when you're turning down all those strange suggestions.

Clearly, it's very important that you should never, ever reach one of these meeting places too early or, in other words, not late

*I've spent whole years of my life hanging around outside
public lavatories waiting for the others.*

enough. Law Three of Subsoccer needs to be observed most strictly, and not only to prevent frostbite, moral decadence and so on. Subsoccermen are in some ways an unimaginative lot, at least when it comes to travel arrangements, and several teams often use the same pick-up point at various times during the hours before kick-off.

A PICK-UP IN PUTNEY

I was once stupid enough to arrive at a spot somewhere in Putney a full ten minutes before I should have been there. In my defence I can only say that it was many years ago, before I'd been fully initiated into the mysteries of Subsoccer. I stood there for perhaps thirty seconds before a battered vehicle that had once been some sort of Vauxhall screeched to a stop inches from my feet. A distraught figure in a dinner jacket jumped out and seized me by the shoulders.

'Thank God I've found you,' he gasped. 'I've been driving round and round these damn' streets for hours. We're four short, but if we can hold out until half past three Gerry's father's coming, and he used to live next door but one to Bobby Charlton!'

It took me fifteen minutes to convince the poor man that I'd never actually played for Real Raynes Park before and didn't want to start now. He was so disappointed that I had to take him to a pub for a drink. As it happened the story had a happy ending: we discovered that we only had ten ourselves, so he came and turned out for us instead. To be fair, he was a little worried about leaving his own side short, but the team sophist soon persuaded him it didn't matter, as you weren't allowed to start a game with less than seven men, anyway. No true sub-soccerman would ever believe that, however, and I prefer to think of Real Raynes Park lining up with a goalkeeper, back four, and nothing else at all. I'm sure they would still do more attacking than a couple of First Division sides I could name.

A NEWCOMER IN CARDIFF

A friend of mine had a similar experience, but things ended rather differently. It was supposed to be his first game for us, but when we all met – outside the prison in Cardiff – he was nowhere to be seen. We hung about for an hour or so and finally left, spitting and swearing, all except the team optimist who kept insisting that we shouldn't be too hard on him since he might be lying in a mangled, bloody heap beneath some bus. Only those who know just how rarely anyone even sees a bus in Cardiff can fully appreciate the lunacy of this. In any case, I think we picked up our eleventh man in a traffic jam, and that was that.

Well, almost. I saw my friend in a pub a couple of weeks later and managed to work out what had happened. He had of course been kidnapped, whisked away to play for another team altogether, after arriving at the prison those fatal few minutes early. Realising I wasn't there myself, he assumed I'd been dropped but was too ashamed to tell him. I spent the whole night and most of my money trying to explain that he'd played for the wrong side – he never was much good at names. Naturally, he stayed where he was, and did very well as an accidental recruit. In fact, he only just escaped being signed by Newport County, which really does underline the perils of punctuality.

Law Four
No Subsoccer motorist is capable of following a given car over a distance greater than twenty-five yards under any circumstances whatever.

Assuming, for a moment, that everyone finally reaches the meeting point on roughly the right day – which does sometimes happen – it might be thought that the worst is behind. There's the game itself to ruin everything, of course, but surely all the rest will now run like clockwork, until kick-off time at least. In fact, all the rest surely won't, because this is where the fun really starts.

Most of the troubles, indeed, are only just beginning, and most of them can be laid at the door of the motor car. Almost literally. Subcars seem to be especially designed to allow just one of their doors to open on any particular day, and that's not the only way in which the coming of the horseless carriage has been disastrous for the subgame.

Once upon a time, I'm told, in the good old days of Subsoccer (and there must have been a few of them, surely), everything did run smoothly once the team managed to meet. Call me a hopeless romantic, but I see hordes of cloth-capped subsoccermen – everyone was cloth-capped then – with those gigantic boots slung round their muffled necks, milling about all over Britain. I see them crowding cheerfully onto trams from New Cross to Nottingham and I see them being ferried, cramped but safe, to their very own bit of bog. I see it all being so simple, then, but I don't see it that way now.

First of all, our old friend the crazy captain, secretary, manager or mad masochist has to work through complex mathematical equations to try to fit the necessary number of bodies into the available cars. This is always complicated by: a) obscure mechanical defects, and b) pathological personal obsessions, all of which surface just as the leader is slipping his calculator back into his pocket. It is then that voices are raised – some pained, some plaintive, and some simply panic-stricken.

'Sorry, only one in the back this week. The offside hyperameter (or whatever) is on the blink and the old girl just couldn't take it.'

Or, 'You don't seriously expect me to wear a jacket with a colour like this in an Escort that looks like that!'

Or (more frequently), 'My God! I'm not going with Tom again! He nearly killed us all in the Blackwall Tunnel last Saturday! I won't go! I won't go, I tell you!'

All this tends to cause even more of a delay, but finally the cars do move off in a straggling procession. And that really is the cue for chaos.

TRAVELLING HOPELESSLY

All we now need for the team to arrive safely at whatever ground they're going to is for each vehicle to follow the one in front. Simple – but impossible. For, as Law Four of Subsoccer tells us, 'No Subsoccer motorist is capable of following a given car over a distance greater than twenty-five yards under any circumstances whatever'. This is partly due to defective eyesight, partly due to awful driving, but mostly due to the unshakable conviction of all subroad-users that they know the best and quickest route to every subground in existence. This belief is quite without foundation. As far as I know, the entire forward line of one of my old clubs is still driving round the Bracknell one-way system; and the match ended five years ago. In fact, if you're ever unlucky enough to ask a subsoccerman for directions, the safest course of action is to do the complete opposite to what you're told. At least you will then know when you are lost.

CONVOY DUTIES

Obviously, in the face of these appalling difficulties, certain counter-measures must be taken if any members of the subside are ever to reach the ground at all. Otherwise you will find roadworks, traffic lights, miners' rallies, little old ladies, lunatic children, low-flying aircraft, suicidal animals and even circus parades, all joining forces to scatter the team to the winds. A fairly simple move is to put the slowest car in front, on the basis that no one can then get left behind; if they are, they can always catch up with the lame duck chugging doggedly along up ahead. Using this method, it once took us three hours to drive four miles through North London, but at least we did arrive with the full eleven. Unfortunately, our right back pulled a muscle taking off his trousers, so we played short anyway.

A less drastic approach, but one which does bring different problems, is for the captain/secretary/masochist to commandeer the nippiest car and shuttle back and forth along the length of the convoy. This means he can collect stragglers and set them back on the right road, rather in the way destroyers shepherded troop carriers across the Atlantic. It does call for plenty of nerve, patience, petrol and good plain luck on the part of the whipper-in, but even that is sometimes not enough. A friend of mine once played for a team run by a rally driver who adopted this scheme for a couple of weeks. Then, one day, after guiding the whole side to the ground, he got hopelessly lost himself within the final thirty yards and ended up playing hockey fifteen miles away.

A DEATH MARCH TO MATCHES

The very finest means of warding off all these dangers to the sub-team, however, must without doubt be the one discovered, quite accidentally, by another of my old clubs. (I have many old clubs. Sometimes I wonder why this is.) We had survived several potentially disastrous away trips entirely unscathed, and had begun to wonder just how we had managed not to lose anyone for so many weeks. I was in the captain's car – a massive black limousine, probably built for an American gangster – when we learned the reason. We had hit a spectacularly nasty jam near Hammersmith Bridge, and conditions seemed ideal for jettisoning at least half of the team; then, all of a sudden, the policeman on point duty stopped all the other traffic and waved us through. He then waved through the rest of our column, and took off his hat as he did so.

There was a stunned silence inside the car as we raced away, until someone gave a strange laugh and cried, 'My God! He thought we were a hearse!'

He was right. After that we carried on pretending to be a funeral for the rest of the season, and by April we were even forming up for the cortège to drive to home matches, which seemed the only way of ensuring that we kicked off some time before six o'clock. Unfortunately the captain finally pushed his luck that little bit too far. He threw away his James Hunt-style peaked cap and took to wearing a black topper; not only that, he started putting flowers on the roof and bumper. People must have thought the entire population of Wimbledon was dying off one by one of some horrible plague. At last the local undertakers realised the whole thing was bogus and threatened to sue; so we were forced to abandon the whole brilliant deception. Still, it was wonderful while it lasted.

It also convinced me that some sort of role-playing along these lines is the answer. Cars could, say, be disguised as armoured cars, or even tanks, with the players pretending to be the Territorials out on manoeuvres – there's plenty of scope. I can't really say, however, that I recommend the idea Cardiff City came up with a season or so back, when they purchased a plane and began to fly to away matches. This wasn't all that successful, since they ended up with a ten-seater: and they had only gone out and bought it because the Press kept saying they needed a couple of good wings.

It is possible, of course, that this book itself will prove to be of some help. Surely other motorists will now realise what's going on when they see four or five cars tagging each other from lane to lane as kick-off time comes nearer. Surely they will now do

We carried on pretending to be a funeral for the rest of the season.

their best to get out of the way. This would be a real bonus on Sunday mornings when, despite the relatively light traffic, sub-soccermen are even more likely than usual to lose themselves – probably due to all the exertions and excesses of the night before. Still, I must admit that driving to Sunday games does make you feel rather proud to be part of a Subsoccer convoy. There can be little to match the sense of shared power as half a dozen of you roar through the silent streets, scattering milkmen and newspaper boys, before screeching to a stop in the car park of the local sports centre. For some reason there is an odd feeling of being in the US Cavalry.

Law Five
No matter how big they may seem, all Subsoccer dressing-rooms are too small.

Once he's actually at the ground, the subsoccerman is on his own. Not quite literally, of course. It is an accepted fact that most sports, and all subsports grounds in the British Isles, have been placed in the most inaccessible spots known to man; even so, just enough of any subteam will always find the one in question to start the game. And, let's face it, anyone lucky enough to get utterly and completely lost never has to play and suffer anyway. It's always the poor fools who dribble in just in time who take the real pasting. And their first test is their ability to survive the dressing-room.

UNDRESSING
There was a time when most subclubs had no such thing as a dressing-room, but the era of open-air changing does seem to be

passing. This comes as a great relief to players who found that other sporting activities were affected by all that prolonged exposure of vital organs to the elements. Not that this is always totally necessary, since it's not only the rugby boys who like to end evenings by going in for unilateral declarations of nudity. Readers who may have seen the centre forward of one of my London sides flashing at startled motorists on the A3 will testify to this. He still claims he was looking for the ditch – but on the central reservation?

To be fair, most submen are not quite such exhibitionists, but none of us has ever been able to be too modest on that score. Two of my friends in Cardiff once narrowly escaped being summonsed for indecent exposure, caught in mid-strip when a middle-aged lady came round a hedge at just the wrong moment. We saw her hanging about near the same hedge for a few weeks afterwards, but we were too young to catch on. Anyway, the outbreak of dressing-rooms on a wider scale has changed all this, even if it's not always for the better.

To begin with, they are all cold and draughty, which makes them even more dangerous, in a sense, since the body's natural defences are relaxed under the illusion of warmth. At least one in three of the windows will be broken, there is always one less coat peg than there are players – even if you turn up with ten one week and seven the next – and the door never quite closes.

But it is the smallness indicated in Law Five that is perhaps their worst single feature, and also the one that accounts for the total lack of team spirit in the subgame as a whole. I defy you willingly to lay down your life for the man next to you when you've just seen him sit on your new cords after trampling all over your leather jacket in boots that haven't been cleaned for three years. Especially if he then goes on to punch you in the eye as he squeezes himself into his smelly old jersey. At one time, changing in a subroom provided useful practice for those stunts where people tried to cram as many bodies as possible into telephone kiosks. Since everyone who used to do that now seems to go jogging instead, the pastime has slipped right out of fashion, and there's nothing left to be said in its favour at all.

BLACK HOLES

Naturally enough, the home team will always use all this to their own advantage. They will be sure to choose the less small (it would be misleading to say larger) of the rooms available; they will also make certain that they have an absolute minimum of actual changing to do. This explains the odd mixture of dress – jacket, shirt, tie, football shorts, football socks, suede shoes, etc. – to be seen in the streets around subgrounds at most hours of the weekend.

It is important to accept the most minute dressing-room with something approaching good grace. Any complaint is invariably quite useless and will be met with bland, blank, idiotic but well-rehearsed smiles; besides, it also wastes breath, something no subsoccerman can afford to squander. No, much better to make a careful note of clubs that go too far in the Black Hole of Calcutta stakes and take revenge in the return fixture. A classic device that allows you to do just that involves persuading an entire side that they must change in a single toilet cubicle. In this way, several of them may be permanently damaged before the team creep rushes up to apologise for the dreadful misunderstanding.

NO-GO AREAS

No toilet in any Subsoccer ground, by the way, ever has any paper. Again, this is the result of clever planning by the home side who will have secret, private supplies for themselves. Most subsoccermen eat huge meals of fish and chips before every game, so at least one trip inside is vital, and this can very easily turn to torture. There can be few more frustrating experiences than to collapse onto the seat in relief, only to perceive with growing horror the lack of the all-important paper. I have seen grown men physically restrained from ripping open their wage packets as desperation drives them to despair.

Obviously, there are several neat dodges to be worked around the toilet, one of the finest being the self-locking door which can't be opened from the inside. I was once the victim of this ploy on the ground of an Isthmian League club, no less. I was just settling down to spend an afternoon with *The Sun* – it was January, and the afternoons were very short – when I was dramatically rescued by our curry-mad left back who had dashed back to deal with a pre-match meat madras. The true connoisseur, however, really should dismiss this kind of gambit as faintly distasteful and also slightly cheap – even though, in another sense, it may actually turn out to be rather expensive. Respect for private property just isn't what it used to be, and nowadays the prisoner may simply kick his way out. I myself feel the whole zone should in fact be declared a no-go area. As far as hostilities are concerned, anyway.

DROPLETS AND DOBIES

While on a more or less sanitary subject, it's probably as well to say a word about the subshower. As with dressing-rooms and toilets, subshowers should be treated with massive suspicion on away trips and turned (literally) to enormous advantage at home. True, the shower can't normally be used to maim the opposition before the game, for obvious reasons (although I did once see a man ordered to wash before the referee would let him onto the pitch – he was a sewer cleaner). But even after the match, all showers on strange grounds should be regarded with extreme caution – they may try to nobble you for next time. Improved plumbing techniques mean that most now work, i.e.

they spurt water, but British technology has not yet quite caught up with the idea that some type of temperature control is more than an optional extra. The result of this is that most sub-showers defy all known laws of physics, veering wildly between boiling and freezing points with no stopping-place in between.

The doyen of the breed is an infamous College Pavilion in South-West London, which sends a steady stream of patients to the nearby hospital suffering from 1) hypothermia, and 2) second-degree burns. At least it keeps the doctors on their toes, I suppose.

I need hardly add, I hope, that the subshower, for all its risks, is still far, far safer than the plunge bath. Anyone who has seen a whole team stricken by the dreaded Dobie's Itch (I swear this is a medically attested disease) forgets all that all-in-together non-sense about cameraderie and never jumps into the water until he's quite certain where everyone else has been and who they've been there with. You have been warned.

Law Six
No pre-match warm-up ever ends before the players are
freezing cold.

Once the subsoccerman has survived the savage toilet and twisted himself, contortionist-style, into the sacrificial garments he will wear for the next couple of hours, he should sprint, stag-ger or stumble outside and look at the pitch. At once he will es-tablish a very obvious but important fact: the goalposts will or will not be in place. If he sees the woodwork glinting prettily against the surrounding morass, he can heave a sigh of relief, stroll back inside and, perhaps, smoke half a packet of cigarettes while hanging comfortably from a coat peg. If, on the other hand, nothing breaks the soggy monotony of the no-man's land in front of him, he must race back to the changing-room and drag out enough bodies to help him put up a set of posts.

Now I can hear those new to the subgame gasp in horror at the idea of ever volunteering for anything, especially this. Veteran subsoccermen, however, will already be nodding their dented foreheads in agreement.

Putting up the posts on a cold, wet, windy day is, I admit, extremely unpleasant. Apart from the fact that it's all a little too much like hard graft — and is it me, or is all that wood really becoming heavier season by season? — there's the frustration, too. Even when the things are up, they are never really more than a poor imitation of the gleaming white contraptions you see at Wembley. The local population always seems to use one of the holes meant to take the uprights as a spare dustbin, while amateur oil prospectors apparently sink test shafts down the other. As a result, the crossbar is often twelve feet high at one end, while at the other it just about reaches the knee. Wasting all that time and effort in such hopeless construction efforts isn't exactly the best way to build up for a game, but the point is that if you don't put them up, you'll have to take them down. And that really is painful.

Despite the fact that gravity is now on your side, this should be avoided at all possible cost. As you fumble with numb fingers to force square posts into round holes (this does actually happen) you can at least console yourself with pathetic fantasies of sending the ball speeding between them. On the other hand, there can be few more abject states of depression than the one you sink into as you pull the rotten things down again when you've lost sixteen-nil and been booked for laughing at something one of their lot said to the ref. It's at times like these that shattered hulks of men have been seen trying to use their jockstraps to hang themselves from the crossbar.

TIGHT CORNERS

It is possible, of course, that you will be unavoidably delayed in
the dressing room – by straining vital muscles, for instance, as
you jam yourself into your jersey and attempt to force your head
through an armhole. When this happens, you may find you
simply can't help, or even pretend to help, with the goalposts.
Quick-thinking subsoccermen, whose reactions have not been
totally devastated by drink and debauchery, can still wangle a
way out of the post-match demolition duties. With luck they will
be able to grab the corner sticks (note that they never, ever have
flags on their ends) and march purposefully around the pitch.

Another word of warning. Although they may impale the occasional tea-lady as you reel through the pavilion, subcorner
sticks are especially designed not to stand upright in the ground.
Because of this, it's simply not sensible to risk personal injury by
trying to force them into the earth. And it's all wasted effort, in
any case, because if they did stick in, wingers would only pull
them out to take corners.

Some years ago I was told that this rational and widespread
practice is actually against the Laws of Association Football. I
suppose it may be, although there's certainly nothing in the
Rules of Subsoccer on the subject. Anyway, no subref standing
in the goalmouth can see far enough to be sure who's taking the
kick, let alone what may happen to any stray bits of wood here
and there. I have a friend who swears that in one game on a
misty afternoon out in Ongar, a friendly spectator with a particularly strong left foot took all his side's corners in the second
half, until he actually scored with one of them. The referee did
seem a little suspicious after that, since everyone slunk sheep-
ishly back for the restart rather than joining in the usual conga/
hakka/gang-bang that generally greets a goal.

WARMING UP

By the time the goalposts and corner sticks are standing and/or lying where they should be, the subsoccerman has actually come tantalisingly close to starting the match. However, before the satisfaction that comes with the music of the kick-off whistle, he must still face the terrors of what is laughingly called the warm-up.

In proper soccer, this dangerous period is very properly kept to a minimum. To prevent pulled muscles, the players go through a series of yoga-style stretches in the comfort of their warm, pleasant, and most of all *big* dressing-rooms. When they do appear out there on the pitch, usually with about four footballs each, they split into small groups, stroke passes back and forth across the turf, and generally behave in a very polished, businesslike manner. In the few minutes before the referee walks out to start the game, everything moves with the precision of a well-oiled machine.

There is the odd exception, of course. I remember one bearded, buccaneering defender who seemed to play for just about all London's League clubs in turn. He always trotted down the tunnel that little bit late, and then jogged doggedly round and round one half of the field, totally refusing the slightest contact with any stray football that came his way. The ball – any ball – he seemed to be telling the centre forward, really wasn't his main target.

If he had been a subsoccerman, in fact, he would have been jogging doggedly for a very long time. This is because no sub-game ever begins when it's supposed to, due to the late arrival of the players, the referee, the park-keeper, the kit, the ball or whatever. This explains Law Six: 'No pre-match warm-up ever ends before the players are freezing cold.' Every now and then these delays reach absurd proportions. I once shivered through a warm-up that eventually lasted longer than the match itself, while the other lot waited for six of their team to turn up. (They had somehow got involved in the Lord Mayor's Show.) And then they won. Indeed, you must accept that in cases like this, the side that finally totters onto the pitch, hopelessly confused and in total disorder, always will win. The other team will not only be suffering from frostbite and terminal boredom; they will also be under the very dangerous misapprehension that they now have a moral right to victory. This is quite fatal. Unless they score at least five goals in the first fifteen minutes they will begin to rail against the malignant fates and leave themselves open at the back.

Late appearance on the pitch can obviously be used by the cunning as a simple but very destructive dodge. The only worthwhile response, if you find yourself on the wrong end of this tactic, is to march straight back to the dressing-room. Make it perfectly clear to the referee that you will now come out again when they do, and not a moment before. This does, admittedly, lead to complicated stand-off, sit-in situations, which can only be resolved through complex negotiation and compromise. Usually it ends with huge defenders squeezing through a tiny door in massive pairs to heal wounded pride. But it must be better than losing before you even begin.

WEARING DOWN

Even if the warm-up lasts no more than a couple of minutes, which it never does, there are dangers of a different sort. Another name for all this pre-match agony is the kick-in, which is not only a lot more accurate but also provides a clue to the problems it brings. Most subclubs simply don't possess unlimited supplies of footballs; many are lucky to possess even one. This means the kick-in is often conducted with a kind of antique object that seems a cross between a cannon ball and a Christmas pudding.

To start with, there is a furious, frantic scramble to get hold of the horrible, lumpy blob. This battle is traditionally marked by tackling of a ferocity never reproduced in the match itself. Timid little bank clerks who usually creep inoffensively along the wings, assistant librarians who wouldn't challenge a determined butterfly in midfield, will both be seen to flatten bricklaying centre halves. And it's even worse if they fail, and defenders come out on top. Obese, immobile full backs, who have not scored for eighteen seasons, insist on shooting practice, muttering vaguely about overlaps. Their idea of this is to place the ball carefully about three yards out and then blast it fiercely at the navel of the cringing goalkeeper.

To be fair, whenever there do happen to be a few spare footballs about, the whole team will do the same, crashing one blockbuster after another into the poor keeper. Some shout and scream as they do so. It's all part of the fantasy that drives them to play at all, of course, although that hardly helps the poor man in the way, for all too often the upshot is a shell-shocked keeper with fingers like a bunch of bananas.

More than any other player, the poor Aunt Sally between the posts needs all his natural instincts of self-preservation to survive the kick-in and make the kick-off. I am convinced that the surprisingly large percentage of high-scoring games in Subsoccer is not the result of marvellous marksmanship on the part of the forwards at all. It's actually caused by so many subkeepers being injured before the match and sent out to slouch along the wing. Their jerseys are then forced on reluctant replacements, who spend the afternoon sulking and letting in Weetabix goals.

Naturally, it goes without saying that anybody who really does want to stay there as the last line, or simply happens to be keen to retain the use of his hands, should keep a very close watch on his team-mates at these times. If he catches the crazed glint in the eye that generally signals one of the mad assaults, he

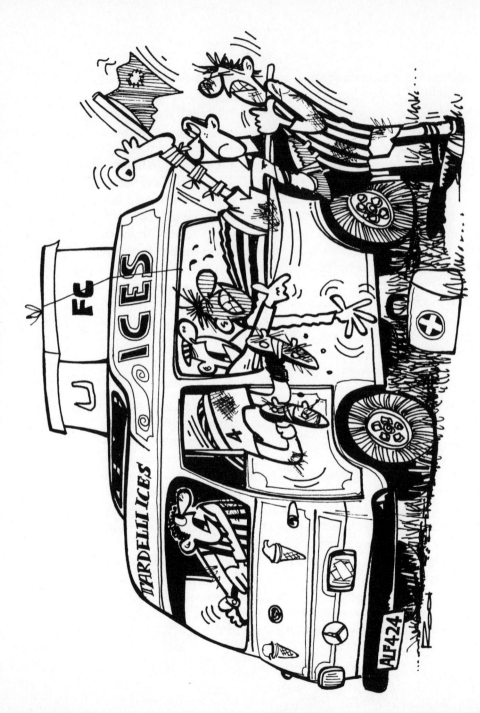

'They always get you in the end,' he spat out, lying there
...

should stride with dignity to a point immediately behind the goal and stand there instead. He should stay there, ignoring all jibes about parentage, manhood, sexual dexterity and so on, and refuse to return until the kick-off.

A TRAGEDY IN TEDDINGTON

Once the warm-up is over, the subsoccerman has all but made it. He has defeated the grand coalition of forces – human, animal, vegetable and mineral – that have joined together in the bid to keep him from his rightful place. It's a time for satisfaction, because once the game actually begins, he's extremely unlikely to feel anything like as contented again. Still, those few seconds just about justify it all. Why, if someone slices a clearance into that river over there, he may even go two whole minutes into the match before making his first awful blunder and wilting under the abuse of the rats who pretend to be on his side.

A final word of caution to captains: those last moments before the lurch into action can still be fatal. I shudder at what happened to an old skipper of mine in Teddington on a day when we were, astonishingly, about to kick off with eleven men. The referee had just called the supremo to the half-way line when, out of nothing, a bloodcurdling scream split the smoggy air. Both sides dashed to the centre circle to find our leader stretched out on the ground, clutching a very strange looking arm and moaning feebly. For some reason the ref had asked him to spin the coin, and he'd dislocated his elbow trying to toss up. He had to be taken to hospital, so we played with ten after all.

I shall never forget his last words, grated out between gritted teeth as he was loaded into an ice-cream van. (I think there was an ambulance strike.)

'They always get you in the end,' he spat out, lying there among the raspberry ripples.

Sad, but true. You can never be too careful.

2
THE GAME

Law Seven

The ability to talk about the game in the bar will be in inverse proportion to the ability to play the game on the pitch.

Experience, animal cunning, and the survival instinct usually mean that the determined subsoccerman takes the field at some stage during the match. Once he's there, however, once he becomes part of the general mayhem, he finds it desperately difficult to work potentially ingenious dodges into the game itself, simply because of the complete and utter chaos going on all around. This averagely mad anarchy rules out not only an awful lot of individual initiative, but also all chance of persuading any subteam to adopt anything like an organised system of play.

This can mainly be traced to the feeble simple-mindedness of most of the players, and their dog-like obedience to anyone actually able to talk about the game. A famous First Division manager was once quoted as saying he found it easier to work with footballers who weren't all that bright; but even he might have felt that subsoccermen sometimes take things a little too far.

Take formations. Any coaching by a Subsoccer supremo on 4–2–4, 4–3–3, 4–4–2 and so on, will only end with the team arranging itself into neat little lines across the pitch. They will then march up and down in strict order, smiling pathetically towards the touchline, while the other lot stroll through for shooting practice. The whole thing is rather like those displays given by massed bands at the Cup Final. Without the music, of course; instead you hear the strangled groans of the subsupremo who stands shuddering at the side of the pitch.

In fact, these systems remind you even more of those football games in amusement arcades – the kind with little wooden players, impaled on steel rods, who spin and somersault and sometimes smash the ball towards the other end. Come to that, the subplayers might do better if they were impaled on steel rods, too. At least they could all kick at the same time, and even make the occasional move sideways.

THE EXTRA MAN

The only formula of this type that ever impressed me was the result of a quite breathtaking fraud engineered by a man I heard of in Australia. He was teaching in Sydney in the days when soccer down under was just about peeping out of the marsupial pouch, and somehow or other came to run a local side. In the past, they had never been too successful, but now, all of a sudden, they started to win everything in sight.

They sewed up the Outback and District League (or whatever) by a street and picked up a couple of other trophies as well. They reached the final of the biggest cup competition in the area and won that, too – very easily, what's more – amazing the crowd by the way they constantly created the extra man. When the team trooped up to collect their medals from the mayor, the poor man became quite flustered to find there weren't enough to go round. A quick recount, however, showed there were indeed eleven trophies; unfortunately, there were more than eleven men.

The resourceful sub-boss had played a daringly original 4–4–3 all through the season (he later claimed he'd simply forgotten to include the goalkeeper), only to be caught out right at the death.

It was a terrible shame, of course, that the twelfth-too-many couldn't somehow have been smuggled away in the celebrations at the end. I suppose the subcoach has to take some of the blame for that – but I still feel he might have made a real go of the England job.

PICKING YOUR SPOT

Strangely enough, the fact that it's more or less impossible to use any sort of mathematical shorthand in the subgame spotlights another area where the sport sometimes runs parallel to trends at the very highest level. Remember Total Football? Many people said that the style adopted by Johan Cruyff's great Dutch side of the 'seventies was the only way to play. Many people say it still is. All of which is very pleasing to the subsoccerman, since Total Football has been played by subteams since the dawn of history, and possibly even before.

When they have the ball (rare), everyone attacks; when the other lot have the ball (also rare), everyone defends; when nobody has the ball (not rare at all), everyone tries to get it. Small boys play this way in school playgrounds; so do soccer-mad dogs when they become tired of chasing motor cars and chase footballs instead. It used to be called kick-and-rush, but Total Football does sound so much nicer.

This strange attraction, which draws subsoccermen after the ball the way knights in armour were once drawn after the Holy Grail, does, in fact, make picking a side that much easier. At least, it does when it comes to deciding who should play where – deciding who should play at all is something else again.

Duties, roles, and positions can be worked out along very simple lines, all based on what people do least badly. Putting it briefly, less old, less slow players should be put in attack; this is important, since they will have further to run to get back to their own half once the ball is inevitably lost. Less young, more slow players should be put in defence; because of the chronic lack of speed, they will hardly ever have enough time to trundle so far upfield that they leave their own penalty area completely empty. The oldest and slowest player of all should be put in goal, for obvious reasons. And players who turn out to be older and slower still should be shot, otherwise they will never cease to whine, whinge, and generally be a nuisance. If they refuse to be shot, they should be transferred to other unsuspecting subclubs; or even turned into subrefs and carefully bent to order.

BEST LEFT ALONE

Nobody should ever play on the left-hand side of the pitch. I realise that may sound rather drastic, especially to those with fond memories of, say, Jim Baxter, Rivelino, Liam Brady and so on. The point is, however, that experience, often painful, has proved to me that all subsoccermen are completely, irreversibly, hopelessly right-footed. Indeed, most proper soccer players in the country seem to be the same. Does this reflect, somehow, what we're always being told is the inherent conservatism of the British race? I do not know. A friend of mine, admittedly not the most committed EEC man I've ever met, swears all left-footed players are snatched from their prams soon after birth and spirited abroad by swarthy, sinister men with funny hats. Was Gento himself kidnapped outside a Sheffield Sainsbury's before he was old enough to say no to a plate of *paella*? I wonder.

My idea of outlawing the left altogether is, I admit, rather revolutionary, but it really is by far the kindest way. I've lost count of all the hideous, horrible, and wholly self-inflicted injuries I've seen suffered out on that dreary wasteland; I've lost count of the number of knees I've seen twisted into corkscrews by men trying to cross from the left with the right foot. I remember one awkward forward who reached the goal-line, tore every tendon and ligament in his right leg in the effort to centre, fell over, attempted to head the ball along the ground into the middle (breaking his nose) and ended up lying twitching in the mud. He then threw the ball into the six-yard box and crawled out of the game for good.

Sharper-minded readers may have realised that if two sub-teams decided to declare the left out of bounds at the same time, the result would be rather novel. Each side would take it in turns to shuttle the ball carefully along its deserted right wing, turn left, and then lose it somewhere in front of goal. It could then be slowly moved, by the same route, to the other end, before being lost again. In other words, play would go round and round in circles, probably ever-decreasing circles, until it disappeared up its own centre spot. Perfection.

THE UNICORN

Naturally enough, the rare, epoch-making discovery of, for instance, a real genuine left winger brings fame, fortune, success, alcoholic poisoning and so on to the lucky lad. Actually, I often wonder if there might not be more of these people about than we think. The point is that nobody ever bothers to look for them now, since they believe they no longer exist, rather like the unicorn. When they do come along they often turn up by sheer chance, but even then we hardly ever keep them as they always tend to develop chronic bronchitis. This is because nobody ever gives them the ball; long years of left-wingerless Subsoccer have convinced the others that the strange, isolated figure shivering out there on the edge of the pitch must be some sort of mirage. They tend to die young, or write sonnets on their solitude. Sometimes they do both, often during the game itself.

Amazingly enough, one of my old teams, a university old boys' side, once had two left wingers at the same time, neither of them at all bad (although their sonnets could have been better). We also had a sort of right winger, and that meant we had a problem: whom should we not pick? After endless debate, we solved our difficulty quite brilliantly by not 'not picking' anybody, and took the field with three wingers. This did not work.

Players like this, you see, really do need the security of a nearby touchline, otherwise they become quite upset and behave very strangely, wandering about in midfield sucking their thumbs and so on. So it was with Keith, who found there just weren't enough wings to go round. He spent about twenty minutes roaming aimlessly in the middle of the pitch and then, all of a sudden, fixed his eyes on the half-way line. He ran back and forth along this for the rest of the game, doing less than nothing for our lot but often bumping into the referee, who was very unimpressed. We lost by quite a lot that day.

TALKING TACTICS

Clearly, then, all systems, strategies, game-plans, counter-ploys and so on should be no more ambitious than those I've suggested. People who arrive at the monthly training session at the local, claiming to be coaches, should be treated with total and absolute suspicion. Good coaches are rare enough in proper soccer, after all, so what can you expect? Anybody at all interested in coaching a subteam must, by definition, be a subcoach; and any subcoach must be a one-time subplayer who is, a) too old, b) too bad, or c) too suspended to actually turn out any longer. So any subside silly enough to put themselves in his hands is likely to, a) lose, b) lose, or c) lose. Just remember Law Seven of Subsoccer, that 'The ability to talk about the game in the bar will be in inverse proportion to the ability to play the game on the pitch'. Perhaps only those lucky enough to have lined up alongside Fleet Street football writers in charity matches know just how true this is.

TALKING NONSENSE
Not that Law Seven means that subfixtures themselves take place in a sort of eerie silence. Far from it. The players compensate for the more or less total lack of crowd noise (a result of the more or less total lack of crowd) by keeping up a constant commentary on what they see happening. There is, without doubt, more meaningless noise in Subsoccer than in any other game, with the possible exception of politics. True, you don't hear too many of those obscure and faintly obscene cries – 'Man on!' 'Tuck in!' 'Drop off!' etc – that you hear in the professional game. But rising above all the desperate panting for breath is a stream of abuse, insult, and general filth that has driven more than one referee to ear-plugs. (They all *say* you're blind, so why not actually *be* deaf?)

A typical exchange between a couple of defenders might go something like this:

CENTRE HALF: You slow –––. You ––– slow –––.
I've seen ––– milk turn faster than you.

RIGHT BACK: –––.

CH: Kick the ––– up in the ––– air next time, you –––.

RB: –––.

CH: If you'd lay off that ––– barmaid you'd be a lot
––– quicker.

RB: –––. What ––– barmaid?

CH: The one with the big ––– in the Angel and Crown.

RB: –––. And she works in the Coach and Horses,
anyway.

CH: You go down there?

RB: Yeah. Nice pint.

CH: Suppose so. But the crisps are always soggy.

RB: –––.

And so on. Now, how could you ever hope to convince two men

like CH and RB (and they are by no means untypical) that they could strike up the trust and understanding you need to spring one of those neat little offside traps?

Law Eight
Goalkeepers go away, but goalkicks don't.

Conventional tactics, then, are out. And even the Subsoccer equivalent – low, mean, cunning tricks and deceptions – are painfully difficult to work into the mad loose-maul of open play. They should be saved, instead, for the Dead Ball Situation (DBS).

These Situations, including the Free Kick Situation, the Corner Situation, the Throw-In Situation, and Other Such Situations, many of them Ongoing, are Very Important Situations. First of all, they bring the chance of a rest. Some time-and-motion expert once calculated that the ball is actually in play for no more than fifty minutes in the average first class match; this can probably be halved in Subsoccer, since there are no packed terraces to throw the ball back. And subsoccermen always seem capable of kicking so much further when they smash the ball into touch. I have never known why.

In any case, the DBS, or Set Piece (SP), does give you an opportunity to impose some sort of order on the chaotic calamities all around. This is where the ruses should be unrolled and the dodges displayed – always remembering, of course, to base these on the obvious shortcomings of the opposition (cowardice, incompetence, vanity, stupidity, etc.), rather than on any silly ideas about your own skill (the ability to kick the ball so that it goes where you want it to go).

THE BIG BOOT
To be strictly accurate, of course, the goalkeeper's kick-out

doesn't really count as a proper DBS or SP at all. It is, however, the time in the game when the ball can be kicked hardest, highest and furthest, and indeed on a particularly bad day these punts may mean the only moments when you make it into their half at all. Now, there's been an annoying tendency, in recent years, for goalkeepers to throw the ball out. This is not at all sensible, since it doesn't go very far, and I've never been able to understand why they do it. I much prefer the good, solid traditions of the average First Division game with both keepers blasting the ball miles up the middle for most of the afternoon. It is then that the gap seems to narrow.

Goalkeepers themselves are only too pleased to slam footballs into the skies in this way. It makes a change, after all, from standing there shaking as the thing comes hurtling towards you. They also believe they might score. Peter Shilton has done it, so has Pat Jennings, and I've even gone close a couple of times myself, especially in windswept outposts like Blackpool. I remember one game near South Shore Airport, when the usual hurricane was breezing up and down the Fylde Coast, when I was easily our most dangerous attacker. We would carefully build up to the edge of their box, and then pass back until I could take a hopeful drop-kick at the far end. I put a couple just over the bar, too.

FA – OK!

Even if the odds may be slightly against a goal from this ploy, it should never be ignored completely. For one thing, a good deal of time can be wasted before the big boot itself – sometimes, in fact, the entire match can drift into a sort of suspended animation. During a particularly fast and frantic affair down in Feltham, I once saw both teams take a very sensible fifteen-minute breather in this way. They had clearly agreed on a tacit non-aggression pact, and twenty players wandered peacefully around the half-way line while the two keepers sailed the ball harmlessly back and forth above their heads.

A word of praise here, by the way, for FIFA, UEFA and – especially – the FA, who have made these stoppages so much easier. In the days when the goalkeeper had to trot briskly through his area, bouncing the ball before kicking it downfield, it was sometimes quite difficult to bring things to a total stand-still. The magnificent four-step rule, of course, changed all that. What with the keeper catching the ball, putting it down, drib-bling it, picking it up, looking at it to make sure it's the same ball he put down, pointing the maker's name in the right direction, waiting for the referee to move the centre forward out of the way, and so on – what with all that, there is now the chance of a really good rest.

And the FA's own, reassessed interpretation of the law has been even better. Over the past couple of seasons, our keepers have had to catch the ball, put it down, and then – and this is the brilliant bit – wait for somebody else to come and touch it before they can move it again! Just a tiny touch, you understand, noth-ing enormous, but the whole thing can take hours, with feints, dummies, counter-feints and counter-dummies by sweepers, full backs, centre forwards, wingers and so on, before someone supplies the necessary nudge. Whole games can go by until the poor keeper can at last go into his dribble, pick up, look, point, wait, etc., routine. So you have to hand it to the FA: I've heard some nasty people say they don't have a clue about soccer, but they obviously have the interests of the subgame very much at heart.

THE LITTLE BOOT

If the keeper (and the ball) soar to the heights with this kind of clearance, however, he (and the ball) are brought right down to earth by the goalkick. Literally. Most subkeepers are quite incapable of kicking it so that it goes up in the air or, indeed, so that it goes any real distance at all. That, of course, is one of the reasons for their being subkeepers in the first place. Never does the dead ball seem more dead, and it would be quite absurd even to talk of turning this one DBS to any sort of advantage. Heroic efforts may get the thing far enough out of the penalty area to avoid a goal against, but that really is about all you can hope for.

I once saw one poor man trying to clear the box no less than twelve times, the ball bobbling along more and more slowly with each miskick, and stopping further and further away from the eighteen-yard line. The subref, probably a sadist or an imbecile – or possibly both – stood just outside, shouting what he might have meant to be encouragement.

'Nearly! Nearly! Hard luck with that one! Have another go!' he called brightly, a lunatic grin on his face. Finally the keeper kicked the ball for a corner, collapsed, and was carried to the bar.

The fact that none of his colleagues offered to take the kick for him didn't mean that the subkeeper was especially unpopular with his team – no more so than subkeepers always are, anyway. No, all subsoccermen realise that the use of outfield players to deal with this deadly DBS simply leaves them in the same state of exhaustion. And for some reason, the kicks themselves will be just as bad. Whole defences can be totally ruined in this way, and I feel a change in the rules really is long overdue. Surely it would be far more reasonable, not to say humane, to demand that the ball should clear, for instance, the six-yard box. Or even the goal-line. As it is, taking goalkicks takes a huge toll of goalkeepers, plunging them into deep depression and finally driving them out of the game altogether. As Law Eight of Subsoccer tells us, 'Goalkeepers go away, but goalkicks don't'.

All this should be forgotten, of course, when it's the other lot's turn to take a goalkick, which can immediately be used to

The whole team should line up on the edge of the penalty area, pointing and jeering, daring the keeper to get the ball over their heads.

advantage. I suggest that the whole team should line up on the edge of the penalty area, pointing and jeering, daring the keeper to get the ball over their heads. I firmly believe league champion-ships can be won in this way.

Law Nine
Nothing ever reaches the far post.

Since subsoccermen belt the ball so far whenever they kick it into touch, throw-ins can be classed with the keeper's punt as a useful time for rest and recuperation; otherwise there seems little to be done with them. Subsoccermen cannot use their hands at all, except to hold beer glasses and interfere with barmaids; and even if they're not that much better with their feet, that doesn't really matter here. I suppose goalkeepers could take pretty fair throw-ins, but to use them for that might be slightly risky. It might also lead to dangerous cases of role confusion, leaving the poor fellows even more bewildered than before.

A few years ago, a team of mine did have a midfield player who somehow developed a long throw. This, he believed, came about when he grew a beard that made him look like Martin Chivers (his great Spurs hero). Actually, it made him look more like Martin Borman, but we didn't have the heart to tell him. Anyway, his throw-in was a beauty, forty yards and as straight as an arrow, a real freak of nature. Sometimes he even reached the far post. This was shattering, since it broke Law Nine of Sub-soccer and left us very confused indeed. But we needn't have worried. The first time he tried it in a match, the referee promptly blew for a foul throw. Anything with a range like that, he announced, simply had to be illegal, even though he wasn't absolutely sure why. We accepted this at once, secretly rather re-lieved, but Martin (names do stick) was distraught. The baffled bearded wonder took the whole thing very much to heart, and never played again. He ran through a whole series of different sports instead, throwing, hurling, putting and tossing discuses, javelins, shots, cabers, hammers, cricket balls, wellingtons, cow-pats and even – once – a traffic warden. In the end he gave the whole thing up and settled for snakes and ladders.

AN ALTERNATIVE APPROACH

Perhaps, after all, there is only one rational approach to the throw-in, and that is to throw the ball straight back into touch – on the basis, you see, that it must be better for the other lot to make a mess of things than for you to do so. This, in itself, demands a fair bit of skill, since referees won't let you do it. I was quite surprised about this the first time I decided to put my ploy into effect. The man kept insisting I take it again.

'But I don't want to. Honestly,' I pleaded.

'But you must,' he explained.

Dismayed to be told he was right, I then took to flinging the ball savagely at my team-mates and finding touch on the rebound. This was only temporarily successful, since they began to run away from me with little shrieks of fright. I then screamed for return passes and made a huge drama out of failing, to my anger, to keep the ball in play. As a variation, I would throw the ball at unsuspecting opponents, hoping to work my way, rugby-fashion, along the touchline, until I could snatch a corner, or an even better DBS such as a free kick. I now feel this may well be the best touch-ploy of all. At times you may be so inaccurate as you aim for one of their side that you accidentally produce a suberb, defence-splitting throw to one of your own.

SHORT ON CORNERS

Corners are much more promising, although Law Nine does present a problem. Luckily, subsoccermen can thank teams like

Tottenham and West Ham for developing the near post corner; nowadays, just about everyone uses it, and subplayers – who couldn't kick it any further, anyway – can easily pretend their corners are dropping short on purpose.

I remember, in my schooldays, there was some sort of unwritten agreement that allowed kind men (usually wearing grey trilbies) to come up and move the ball a few yards in from the actual corner. This helped little wingers no end and, again, is something I feel the game, or at least the subgame, could adopt with advantage.

A few years ago a friend of mine kept finding himself in trouble with the referee on this very point. It was his first match for a senior side, and whenever he was about to take a corner he would wait and look round for one of these kind men in grey trilbies. In the end the referee threatened to book him for time-wasting, and eventually, in the second half, when there was still no sign of a kind man in any sort of hat, he moved it five yards infield himself; he was promptly switched to left back for the rest of his career.

In spite of all this, it is by far the best idea at least to try to belt the ball into the centre; it may then drop somewhere near the edge of the six-yard box, which isn't quite as pathetic as it sounds. No subsoccerman really likes to have to use his head and, with luck and the odd dummy run (all runs in the subgame are dummy runs), it may even bounce towards the middle of the goal. There a wild kick by one side or the other may even put it in.

Real short corners, by the way, with the ball tapped to a man standing no more than a yard or so away, should never, ever be attempted. If they are, the attacking team will never, ever score, but there is every chance that the defending team will.

THE CORNER COUNTER

Defenders lining up to face corners should simply take account of all this and react accordingly. What they should *not* do is flirt with ridiculous refinements such as 'zonal marking'.

I was once in a London University side which adopted this system with quite disastrous results. Each defender was supposed to 'attack' the ball when it came into his 'area of influence', and if this makes our back four sound something like one-man superpowers, it certainly wasn't reflected in their play. The brilliant scheme soon saw us letting in a goal from just about every corner we faced; it became so bad, in fact, that we spent more time worrying about giving away the corners than giving away the goals themselves.

The result was, of course, that nobody ever went anywhere near the ball. All those zones and areas seemed to become amazingly flexible, and the plan's only real advantage was that no one was ever sure who to blame (except the goalkeeper). Team spirit improved for everybody (except the goalkeeper) but we went back to the usual, healthy man-for-man approach – which meant that the entire defence (except the goalkeeper) could scream at our four-foot-nine striker for failing to outjump the seven-foot-one gorilla who'd come up from centre half.

Personally, I feel there is only one ideal form of defence at this DBS, and that is the one used by the two full backs who seem to crouch alertly by the posts. Actually, they are not crouching alertly by them at all, but leaning on them. In this position, they can not only take another quick rest but also make the odd goal-line clearance. When they do this, they can look sadly at the sub-keeper, shake their heads, and trot upfield in a very superior sort of way. They have, you see, done something no one really expected of them, something the keeper should have done himself. Why, it's almost as satisfying as scoring!

Not that very many clearances come about in this way. For

some reason, even only averagely bad subplayers go to pieces completely at such times. Instead of simply letting the ball hit them, which would at least stop it, they insist on trying to kick it away, probably picking a man about forty yards out and trying to find him with a left-footed volley that Maradona might think twice about. Once they do that, it's in.

I have a friend called Nelson who's scored dozens in this way, specialising in tremendous blasts into the roof of his own net. He quite upsets the other side's forwards, who think they've slotted one home but then see him ghost in from nowhere to smash yet another OG. I was once lucky enough to watch Nervous Nelson (as we call him) put three past his own keeper in a college cup final, which must be some kind of record. I know, for I was that keeper.

Even so, I'm still certain that corners should see all eleven players, and not just the full backs, lined up along the line. Five can lean on one post, with the other five leaning on the other, while the subkeeper stands swaying between them. In this way there is more rest (yet again) and also a formidable impression of a fence-defence in front of the goal, which looks very solid, even though it isn't. And that brings us neatly to free kicks.

Law Ten
Each and every defensive wall has a hole in the middle, and so has each and every goalkeeper.

There is not much to be said on free kicks that are too far away from the other lot's goal to justify trying any sort of shot: these should simply be passed straight back to the keeper, even if this means knocking the ball back, say fifty yards. His punt will still succeed in moving it further forward than anything attempted with the dead ball itself (see goalkicks, corners, etc.). It's fairly easy, too, to decide if the kick is in fact close enough to their goal for a shot to be tried. If the opposition line up to form a wall, it is; if they don't, it isn't. This is so, even if you can hardly believe the distances they feel come within the danger zone. You may know how pitifully short your own range is, but if they think you might score, that's at least half the battle. Especially since the poor subkeeper hopping about somewhere on the dim horizon, peering out onto the pitch, really can't have too much idea about what's going on in front of him. Even people like Michel Platini, I feel, benefit from this type of paranoia.

Assuming, then, that a shot is on, and it usually is, what follows should be simple and direct. Literally. The ball should be kicked as hard as possible, straight at the human barrier quivering before it. The wall will then very kindly open up, allowing it to pass through and surprise the unsighted keeper. Afterwards, it will immediately close up again, this time becoming such a solid-looking screen that it's quite beyond belief that anything could ever have got through it. But, of course, it has. Every subwall ever set up has this strange, Red Sea tendency mysteriously built into it. And fear, naturally, is the key.

Nobody can pretend that a football doesn't hurt when it hits you. It does. It hurts a lot. I remember one coaching session at Motspur Park in South-West London when someone did try to prove otherwise, but failed miserably. Pain of that sort, he said, was purely psychological. If you gave a stoical grunt and leaned forward as the kick was taken, the whole sensation couldn't possibly add up to more than a faint tingling. Seven players were psychologically laid out in this way before the disappointed coach admitted defeat.

CRANNIES, HOLES AND CHINKS
The main single reason for the hole in the wall, then, turns on this very natural dread of pain. It could probably be scientifi-

cally proved, by diagrams, equations, and geometric theory, exactly why each and every defensive wall does finally open up. And that is because of the fanatical obsession of its members to protect their – well – their members.

It is quite impossible to create an impenetrable barrier of human bodies when each living brick is struggling frantically to keep both hands over its genitals. What happens is that in all the confusion, with the wall being pulled this way and that, at least one player feels his hands being dragged away from the danger area. At once he opts for self-preservation, frees the arms, hugs the crotch, and opens the gap. Even the team geriatric, who hasn't used the equipment at risk for anything other than sanitation in over thirty years, will sell out the side for his vital organs in this way. In all honesty, who can blame the guilty men? It is only a game, after all, and while it's one thing to lay down your life for your club, it's another thing altogether to lay down those.

Still, in spite of the natural sympathy we all feel at these times, you must always milk such situations for the very last drop of propaganda. The wall itself will make astonishing claims that the ball has been bent extravagantly around it and try to blame the keeper. They may even succeed here, as goalkeepers are generally blamed for everything anyway, so the scoring side must make it quite clear what has actually happened. It's always more useful to convince the opposition that half of them are snivelling cowards than to try to pretend that you yourselves are masters of the swerve and dip. Since most subsoccermen can hardly bend their knees, let alone the ball, they won't believe you in any case. No, accept your own limitations, and just make quite sure the other lot accept theirs as well.

I've always found that the cutting remark works wonders here, and a comment of one of my old team-mates would, I feel, take a lot of beating. He had just seen his shot pass neatly through the middle of a barrier that looked about as massive as the Colorado Dam and settle gently in the net. As a keen amateur dramatics man and desperate ham actor, he was ready with a line from *A Midsummer Night's Dream*, and came in right on cue.

'Thanks, courteous wall,' he intoned, with a sweeping bow.

He told me later that he was about to launch into Bottom's whole speech about crannies, holes and chinks, but it just wasn't needed. I have never seen the morale of a team collapse quite so completely.

The success of this straightforward approach should certainly persuade people to ignore anything more complex in free kick moves. By this I mean the astonishingly complicated and amazingly intricate series of signals, runs, dummies, feints, faints and so on that you sometimes see on *Match of the Day*. They never work – not even on *Match of the Day* – and, once again, can easily end in the other side scoring instead. And don't worry about indirect free kicks, either; you needn't bother about those, for the simple reason that there are no indirect free kicks in Subsoccer. To tell the truth, there is no actual Subsoccer law to that effect, but referees believe, quite rightly, that they would only create even more confusion, and therefore seem to pretend they don't exist. It is possible, of course, that they don't know they actually do exist, but the end result is the same.

DESPERATE MEASURES

When your own side face up to a free kick, however, the boot is quite literally on the other foot. After giving a great deal of thought to the problem, I feel I have finally come up with the answer.

I did consider the cool, calculated bluff, working on the reversal of the wall-erection-equals-shot-possibility theory. That is, refusing to set up a wall at all, in the hope that the opposition will automatically believe they cannot reach the goal. Attractive as this may appear, however, there must come a day when it fails. You can't fool all the people all the time, not even all the people in Subsoccer. Only a cretin would swallow the dodge at a free kick given, say, on the edge of the eighteen-yard box. And you might not be lucky enough to meet a cretin whenever you need one.

No, you really must accept that the wall is more or less necessary, and take it from there. This is why I thought of blindfolds.

Being in a wall is, after all, very much like standing in front of a firing squad, so why not? They could be issued in club colours and worn round the neck when not in use, like a rather raffish cravat. Natty, but in the event, I'm afraid, not very practical. To begin with, they could very easily lead to strangulation in open play. ('Macintosh made a fine run down the right, but was garotted by Smith as he was about to cross.') It's difficult enough to put out a subteam as it is, without seeing half your players shatter their windpipes every week. The famous phrase, 'He was dead choked', could, of course, come to mean something completely different, but that wouldn't really help.

Even if the blindfolds could be worn somewhere else – bandanna-like, for instance, in the fashion of the old banditti (and so 'We was robbed'?) – even then there would be problems. For one thing, it might be difficult to persuade players to take them off once the free kick had been cleared. This would lead to a sort of mad, blind-man's buff soccer that plunged the game even further into the realms of farce.

I did toy, for a while, with the idea of abandoning the blindfold itself but achieving the same effect by ordering the entire wall to face its own goal. Those in the line wouldn't know when to go into their parting of the ways act, and might do so too early or too late, stopping the ball accidentally after all. The pitfall here is that quick-thinking opponents would be sure to take

Blindfolds . . . Being in a wall is, after all, very much like standing in front of a firing squad, so why not?

advantage of the rearguard action and do low, mean things like dribbling around the wall on tip-toe. Also, there could be problems in persuading the more eccentric individuals in the side ever to turn the right way round again. Some might even believe the teams had changed ends, and simply attack the goal (and the goalkeeper) in front of them. I'm sure coaches never think of things like this when they talk about playing the way you're facing.

A DARING SOLUTION

There is in fact only one completely foolproof, cast-iron defensive ploy to put to use when you're on the wrong end of this deadly DBS. In its way it's every bit as daring as the idea of pretending you don't need a wall at all, but besides being daring it could actually work.

It involves putting up your human barrier as usual, but setting it *outside* the goal. The effect is obvious. The other lot, just as sure as you are that the barricade is bound to sprout a convenient hole, will aim at the middle and blast away. The barricade, as petrified as ever, will split as usual. The ball will fly straight through and sail safely wide. Simple, perhaps, but that is so often the stamp of genius.

I need hardly add (but I will) that the wall should be comfortably but not excessively wide of the posts. It would be very nice to watch free kicks being whacked ferociously at the corner flags, but that really is pushing it a little too far. Even a subsoccerman will smell a rat if it bites him on the nose. And one more word of caution: the average dead ball subexpert is so pitifully bad that he will sometimes miss the decoy wall altogether, with a shot so inaccurate that it arrives on target by mistake. Just in case this does happen, goalkeepers who decide to take a quick nap at these times should try to sleep standing up.

PAINS AND PENALTIES

When it comes to penalties, the inaccuracy that can so easily wreck a perfectly decent ploy poses problems of a different sort. Since no subsoccerman can ever be quite certain exactly where the ball will go once it leaves his boot, scoring from the spot does need a good deal of serious study. To be honest, it would be impossible to pretend there is any means of making sure of hitting the net at all, were it not for the fact that a subkeeper stands, shaking, only twelve yards away. But not standing for long.

Just before the ball is kicked, the subkeeper will hurl himself to one side in a dramatic, extravagant dive. As he flies through the air, he will have no earthly hope of actually stopping a shot that goes anywhere near him, since he's far too worried about hitting his head on the post. He doesn't usually dive that far. And in any case, the ball itself will inevitably go the other way. All subkeepers dive the wrong way whenever a penalty is taken.

To be fair, they're not on their own in this; proper, professional goalkeepers, who surely ought to know better, do the same. Most of them earnestly explain that the power and precision of the men they face are so awesome that the idea of actually waiting to see where the ball goes is quite laughable. The whole business has turned into such a guessing game that they could almost cut out the shooting completely and simply toss a coin for the goal instead.

As this wouldn't be quite the done thing, proper goalkeepers apparently build up mental dossiers on regular penalty takers, which leads to mind-boggling 'I know that he knows that I know that he knows that I know … etc.' dilemmas. This, I feel, must be a short-cut to schizophrenia. Subkeepers, on the other hand, have an 'I don't know and he doesn't know' riddle to resolve, but it doesn't matter, the result is still the same. That amateur actor friend of mine always claimed that the character at the end of *Love's Labour's Lost* who pipes up, 'You that way, we this

way', is in fact a spokesman for subkeepers everywhere address-
ing an imaginary ball. And he may be right.

The answer, of course, is to accept that the twain shall never
meet, and use this to the best advantage. Obviously, the keeper
can never stop the ball deliberately: the danger is that it might
accidentally hit him, in spite of his efforts to get out of the way,
or else go wide. There is a solution that avoids both eventu-
alities.

The one place where the goalkeeper will never, ever be is in the
middle of the goal. The sensible subsoccerman, then, will calmly
roll the ball safely into the centre of the net while the poor fellow
in front of him dives hopefully to all points left and right. This is
bound to work, especially since everyone now expects the
keeper to do this, including his own team. It's the only time they
don't sneer, mock and jeer when he lets in a goal. Because of this,
he can almost come to enjoy his part in the whole mad ritual.
I even heard a really shell-shocked subkeeper in one side we
played shout, 'Penalty!' when our centre forward was scythed
down in the box.

BYE-BYE BIRDIE

To be fair, I can't pretend the middle-of-the-road approach is all
my own work. So far as I know, it was invented by a Cardiff City
player called Ronnie Bird, a nippy little forward who, naturally,
played on the wing.

When it came to penalties, he was in a class of his own.
Ronnie would go back about a quarter of a mile, race up to the
ball, and wind up his left foot as if he was about to crash a shot
somewhere into the Bristol Channel. Instead, however, he
would then chip delicately into the middle of the goal, straight
into the space conveniently left by the diving keeper. If the latter
hadn't been diving, but had simply stood still, the ball would
have plopped softly into his lap. It never failed. Then, one day,

he somehow mishit a kick so that it whistled inches above the
turf and into the net about a millimeter inside the post. It was the
best penalty I have ever seen. But Ronnie Bird's confidence was
shattered, and he never took another.

THE SNEAK SHOT
To base both your free kicks and penalties on the wisdom en-
shrined in Law Ten – 'Each and every defensive wall has a hole
in the middle, and so has each and every goalkeeper' – does, I
admit, take a little courage. Anyone too timid to act on this in
the case of the spot-kick – and, to be frank, the odd moral
coward is not entirely unknown in Subsoccer – may plump for
another ploy. In my opinion it is rather a mean, sneaky method,
but I report it nonetheless.

There is, you see, nothing in the rules of either the game or the
subgame to say that you have to shoot at all. It's quite possible to
pass to someone else instead, someone better placed, for
instance. You could even, perhaps, centre from the spot, trying
for a telling cross, in which case the far post would be in real
danger of being reached. So long as at least one of your lot
knows what's going on, there's no reason why this shouldn't
work quite well. But be careful. The opposition will definitely
feel cheated and take horrible revenge, and I can't say I altogether blame them. The two-touch gambit always seems a little
distasteful, rather like going duck shooting with a machine gun.

THE SOFT SELL
When you give a penalty away, the only really effective counter-
measure is equally sneaky. It might not be, if you could somehow guarantee total immobility on the part of the subkeeper,
having him stand quite still to make the inevitable, stationary
save. Unfortunately, you can't. Even if, during the rest of the
game, when you'd be quite happy to see him move, he usually

displays the agility of the average lamp-post. And desperate remedies, such as suspending him from the crossbar, or pinning him to the line with a corner post, will only upset the man even more.

No, taking penalties is all in the mind, and the best defence is in the mind, too. Subtle use of the tongue is the answer, but I cannot stress too strongly that subtlety is very much the watchword here. To bellow, 'You silly ———! You'd have more chance of scoring if you ——— it with your ———!' may let off steam but it's also likely to let in a goal. The subspotkicker has heard it all before, and even the fact that he secretly agrees won't shake him now. It's far, far better to shrug the shoulders, sigh and, before he even places the ball, have a few quiet words with your glum-faced colleagues.

'Heigh-ho (or whatever). That's another goal gone in. This bloke never misses. Never. Never ever. I'm going up to the half-way line to wait for the kick-off. Anyone coming?'

Nobody will ever score a penalty after a build-up like that. Not unless he's stone deaf.

3
The Players

Law Eleven
The game on the next pitch is always better than yours,
even when it is worse.

By now some readers may be wondering why on earth Subsoccer is played at all. Subsoccermen often wonder, too. Obviously, it must all be related to compensation fantasies, but being a do-er, or even a done-to-er, rather than a watcher, does provide one advantage. This reveals itself in sporting conversations, discussions, disagreements, and good plain stand-up rows.

Subsoccermen spend rather a lot of time talking about the game. It is, after all, so much less painful than actually playing it. It's always very satisfying to round off the usual dispute about the thinking behind the latest England team (i.e. whether there *is* any thinking behind the latest England team) with a clever little rhetorical question. Something along the lines of, 'And who do you play for, anyway?' generally reduces opponents to muttering frustration. Sometimes they will attempt to answer back – 'Nobody. But who do you play for? Athletico Amersham, who haven't won for seven years! Huh!' – but luckily this is rare; so even subplayer status can add that touch of smug superiority to your post-match pint.

POINTS ON PINTS
Drinking does play a sizeable part, perhaps even an enormous part, in the proper practice of Subsoccer. It's every subsoccer-

man's aim to spend many, many hours in the pub, not only after the game but before and even, sometimes, during it – although, to be fair, this generally happens only when on tour to the Channel Isles, the Continent, and a small village up in Yorkshire which I'm certainly not going to name here.

While I sympathise with this need for pre-match alcohol as a kind of internal liniment, it can cause problems – on a Sunday morning, for example, when licensing laws make it rather difficult to buy, say, a ploughman's breakfast. An Irish friend of mine always insisted, for this very reason, on going to early mass. Then one day he turned up at the church wearing his kit (we had a long away fixture) and even the priest began to wonder.

In all honesty, pre-game drinking really isn't something the serious subsoccerman ought to encourage. If it increased beyond the present levels – already dangerous enough – we might even see the coming of the pre-match breathalyser. Since many would certainly fail this, due to the after-effects of the night before, this should be avoided at any cost; otherwise an awful lot of us might never take the field at all. An extreme case was a tired and emotional goalkeeper I once saw turn in a quite spectacular performance in an Easter friendly. He gave an immaculate display of handling, holding on to each and every shot he had to deal with, but only as it rebounded from the net behind him. It was one of those games when the keeper let in six and took the blame for seven of them. The poor man just couldn't understand why his side kept kicking off every time he made a save.

A MAN APART

If any member of the weird and unwonderful bunch who make up the average subteam had a right to be driven to drink, it would be the goalkeeper. The game may be played by a totally bizarre collection of beings with just one thing in common – a

We might even see the coming of the pre-match breathalyser — many subsoccermen would certainly fail this.

chronic lack of ability – but for everyone except the keeper there's a kind of comforting acceptance of mutual limitations.

In spite of the delusions of adequacy that spur him to turn out in the first place, neither the centre forward himself nor the rest of the team really expect the bald, fat old fool at number nine to function like Ian Rush. While the centre half and the others in the side certainly don't look for imitations of David O'Leary from the knock-kneed stick insect at number five. But in spite of all this, every single player in the club positively demands that the frail, ageing gentleman between the posts should perform like Peter Shilton.

The reason, you see, is that none of the outfield players has the slightest idea of what any of them should be doing at any particular time. I remember reading that if you could stop *Othello* half-way through and ask Iago just why he was being so nasty to the poor old Moor, he'd have to tell you he hadn't a clue. You could do exactly the same at a Subsoccer match and get exactly the same answer. The difference is that it's all too easy to see what the goalkeeper is meant to do; and most of the idiots in front of him believe they could do it better.

AN AGED ACROBAT

This was underlined by an incident I witnessed one afternoon on Cardiff's Pontcanna Fields, a sort of Welsh Hackney Marshes where you can see a whole gaggle of subgames all going on at the same time. There are so many pitches, in fact, that subforwards have been known to shoot at the wrong goalposts. This hardly matters to the subkeeper, since they generally miss and hit the right set anyway, but it does mean that there's plenty to break his less-than-fierce concentration. Law Eleven of Subsoccer, which tells us that 'The game on the next pitch is always better than yours, even when it is worse', helps explain his problem.

Anyway, that day I stood behind one goal and saw a touching

drama unfold. The right back of the defending team totally mishit a clearance and sent the ball slicing through his own penalty area. There the centre half aimed a wild kick at it and volleyed straight into the face of the left back, knocking him senseless. When the ball rolled to the sweeper, he fell over it, sat on it, and squeezed it backwards to a striker loitering hopefully on the six-yard line. He promptly let fly with a tremendous drive, and then this elderly person in a baggy green sweater took off and soared to his left to touch the ball onto the bar. It rebounded, hit the prostrate left back on the head, and ricocheted towards the goal again. With a superhuman effort, the ancient subkeeper jack-knifed off the ground, flew yards to his right, and managed a stupendous parry. The forward then bobbled the ball into the empty net with most of the defence laid out around him. As the goalscorer broke into demented laughter, the centre half glared back at the beaten keeper.

'For God's sake, Len! Try and hold 'em!' he whined. Then he shook his head at the others, shrugged, and trudged off towards the half-way line.

I was flabbergasted. But I smiled sympathetically at the acrobatic pensioner as I rolled the ball back to him. (It had gone through the net, naturally; subnets, when they exist, are usually designed not to stop any balls that go into them.) He smiled back, for we understood each other. I have rarely felt so close to any human being.

COMPROMISING POSITIONS

In spite of all the trauma and torture he goes through, the subkeeper is still the only player who really has a proper position at all. The others might claim they do, calling themselves full backs, sweepers, strikers and so on, but basically they're all just part of the teeming, seething mass that rolls around the field. Within this mêlée, however, people will insist on pretending to be specialists of one sort or another, and generally fall into several easily-catalogued groups.

The Full Back – The Statue

A worrying trend that's developed in proper soccer over recent years is the tendency of the full backs to move. Once upon a time they simply had to stand there and kick anything that came near the touchline – the ball, the winger, the linesman, the policeman, etc. Now they are expected to go forward and attack as well. This, of course, is not the case in Subsoccer, where overlaps, for obvious reasons, are out. And anyway, subfull backs see what it's like at the other end in the second half, so why do all that running now?

The functions of the full back are, 1) to shout at the goalkeeper; 2) to stand very still in one place, and 3) to show wingers where to turn left for goal.

The Centre Half – The Stooge

The real centre half is often called the king-pin, lynch-pin and so on of the defence. In Subsoccer he is called the ten-pin, since his main aim in life is to knock people over. His preferred target is the other side's centre forward, but he doesn't really mind, and will in fact flatten anyone he's told to flatten. The very best sub-centre half is a stooge, never, ever thinking for himself but doing exactly what the sweeper (see later) tells him. He is quite happy about this, since it usually involves following the centre forward everywhere and kicking him when he can. Sometimes he will even chase him into the toilets after the game. The stooge must be able to head the ball fairly well, but if he can't do this it's quite acceptable to head the centre forward instead.

The functions of the centre half are, 1) to shout at the goalkeeper; 2) to kick the centre forward; 3) not to think, and 4) to obey the orders of the sweeper.

The Sweeper – The Poser

This is probably the pick of Subsoccer's so-called positions, and the one which comes closest to its equivalent in proper football. The sweeper does literally no work whatever. He needn't, in fact, be able to play at all, but he must be able to talk. He can be old, slow, bald, obese, or all four at once, but he must at least look classy. He has to be able to convince everybody else that defending really would be very easy if only the others would do things his way. He must be able to come off the pitch when his side have lost 13–0 and persuade the rest he's had a great game. He must never, ever mark a man and he must never, ever tackle.

The functions of the poser are, 1) to shout at the goalkeeper; 2) to tell the stooge when to kick the centre forward; 3) to talk and 4) to pose.

The Midfield Nonentity – The Headless Chicken

In the old days we didn't have midfield men at all; we had wing halves and inside forwards, and everybody knew where they were. Now, not only in Subsoccer, but everywhere else as well, people who don't really know where to go or what to do play in midfield instead. They run round and round in circles, passing to anybody (especially the opposition) and tackling anybody (especially their own team), and generally behave like chickens just after they've taken the fatal chop. Veteran subsoccermen, in fact, call them headless chickens, but I feel this is a slur on a fine body of birds. At least headless chickens don't squawk.

The functions of the headless chicken are, 1) to squawk at the goalkeeper, and 2) to squawk at other headless chickens.

The Midfield Playmaker – The Fanny Merchant

This is the man who makes the team tick, the player who shapes and crafts his side's carefully-planned moves. Or that's what he says, anyway. The fact is that the team doesn't tick and hardly moves anywhere at all. He claims his talent is his ability to put his foot on the ball, but whenever he does this he falls over. He is openly scornful of midfield nonentities, calling them 'limited', but seems to do even less than they do. He will never play a simple ball if a difficult one, however impossible, can be played instead. The fanny merchant is like the sweeper in that he never tackles, and indeed the two are often seen drinking in a corner together after the match. He, too, talks a fine game, and secretly believes he should be the sweeper himself.

The functions of the midfield playmaker are, 1) to shout at the goalkeeper; 2) to snub the headless chickens, and 3) to plot with the sweeper.

The Midfield Ball-Winner – The Thug

His father is a Mafia hit-man and his mother is a bouncer in the roughest, toughest club in town. He eats nails and fanny merchants. No further description is necessary.

The functions of the thug are, 1) to kick the other side's midfield playmaker; 2) to kick the other side's headless chickens, and 3) to kick anything he hasn't kicked already.

The Winger – The Impostor

Right wingers are almost without exception midfield nonentities who have crept forward, and not real wingers at all. They now run like headless chickens up and down the touchline until helpfully shepherded inside by obliging full backs. (At the statue, turn left.) They cannot run, pass, shoot or cross, but this hardly matters as they rarely get the ball anyway. For some reason, they are always offside. This may be because they are very lonely out there and tend to chase the linesman around, desperate for someone to talk to. Left wingers, of course, are Unicorns (see Chapter Two), and something else again.

The functions of the impostor are, 1) to be offside; 2) to catch cold, and 3) to turn corners into goalkicks.

The Centre Forward – The Target Man

The centre forward is often called the target man, basically because he is there to be kicked by the centre half, and so acts as his target. The two positions are in fact more or less interchangeable – centre halves make (as well as kick) very useful centre forwards, and vice-versa. Target men are in some ways a strange lot, standing about for hours in the other side's penalty area but hardly ever scoring. This may be because they spend so much time with their back to the goal itself, peering hopefully back towards their own team and waiting for the midfield playmaker to blast the ball miles over their head. If it does accidentally arrive at their feet, their control is so awful that it will immediately bounce at least thirty yards away. Target men never take penalties.

The functions of the target man are, 1) to be kicked by the centre half; 2) to score fewer goals than anyone else in the side, and 3) to make goals for the goalhanger.

The Striker – The Goalhanger

This man is an enigma. Season after season he scores more goals than the rest of the team put together, but nobody can ever work out why. It may be because he never does anything else at all. He never runs, as he is lazy; he never tackles, as he is a coward; he never passes, because he is selfish; and he never heads the ball, because he is worried about his hair-do. The striker gets even less dirty than the midfield playmaker, but may moan, groan, and whinge even more. He spends whole years goalhanging around the six-yard box, and would be constantly offside except that the winger is ever further forward and gets offside first. Despite the battering taken by the target man, he himself is never kicked, and always seems very friendly with the other side's sweeper.

The functions of the goalhanger are, 1) to whinge; 2) to keep his shorts clean, and 3) to score more goals than the rest of the team put together.

FOIBLES, FAILINGS AND PHILOSOPHY

It is easy to see, then, why any sanity that does sneak onto a Subsoccer pitch is so often found between the posts. Goalkeepers should be crazy, perhaps, but in the subgame they're just not (although I did know one who married a psychiatrist). Standing out there week after week in the mud and rain, watching the others act out their pathetic fantasies in front of him, the subkeeper simply can't help realising the grim reality beneath the whole ghastly sham. And there's not the slightest chance of labouring under the same delusions himself, since everyone tells him just how awful he is about once every five minutes.

No, the goalkeeper is Subsoccer's philosopher, and it's not difficult to understand why. Man must suffer to be wise, said the Ancient Greeks, and the average subkeeper goes through enough suffering to qualify for a season ticket to that seat on *Mastermind*.

Law Twelve
Most Subsoccer teams constantly start one short, and so do many players.

Apart from the goalkeeper, the majority of subplayers are very obviously short on stoical calm, and sometimes short on other things, too. Now, most footballers do possess the normal number of limbs and so on – they would hardly think of being footballers if they didn't. But this is not always the case in Subsoccer, where people don't let the lack of the odd bit of body stop them turning out. I myself, for example, once played several games behind a back four that had only five eyes.

I promise this is true. It was in the reserve team of what is now a very successful Welsh League club, and I remember the way it went quite clearly. The right back couldn't see out of his left eye, and the left back couldn't see out of his right eye. Neither could the centre half. The sweeper often played as if he couldn't see out of either eye, but that was something else again. To be fair, the defence worked very well together, except when we came up against wingers who liked to cut in and shoot. When they did this, of course, they took both full backs on the blind side.

One of the three one-eyed jacks, as they called themselves, once went through an unnerving experience in a very physical cup tie. Eddie, the left back, picked up a nasty gash to the forehead. He was helped to the touchline, where the trainer tried to patch him up, placing a sponge firmly over the cut, clamping the player's hand on it, and pushing him back onto the pitch. Unfortunately, the gash was over the good eye.

'I can't see! I can't see!' yelled Eddie, stumbling about the field.

'So what?' shouted the trainer. 'You can still kick! Get out there and kick someone!'

COLOURFUL QUIRKS

Oddly enough, many of the defenders I've played with seem to have had problems with their eyesight. (To be fair, they might well say the same about me.) But many of them managed to hide their handicaps for years before being found out. I remember one Sunday morning match in Sunbury when my friend Mick was exposed in this way. As we staggered onto the pitch he looked at the other lot warming up around the far goal and told us we were in trouble.

'Oh-Oh,' he said. 'This isn't too clever. Look at their shirts.'

We did. They were wearing green.

'And look at ours,' he went on.

We did. We were wearing red. This was pointed out to Mick, which was when he came clean.

'Ah, that explains it,' he said cheerfully. 'I never could tell red from green. I'm colour blind. Didn't you know?'

This finally suggested a reason for the eccentric distribution which had always been a part of Mick's game, but it hardly filled the rest of us with confidence. The calling that day was quite bizarre. Instead of the usual 'Here!' or 'Give it to me!' or 'My God! Will you pass!' we had a different sort of shouting altogether.

'Mick! It's Rob! Listen, you know me! I'm on your side! Honestly! All right? Look, I'm jumping up and down and waving my hands in the air! See? Now then, try and kick the ball to me, and . . .'

And so on. We lost.

MISSING IN ACTION

Getting back to bodily shortfalls, I once played against a man who had mislaid another bit of himself. He only had one arm. His side called him the Fugitive and he actually scored a goal against me. Personally I felt he might well have handled as he brought the ball down before belting it in, but I don't suppose many referees would have dared to blow up for it. After all, the Fugitive was living proof of Law Twelve – 'Most Subsoccer teams constantly start one short, and so do many players – especially since the bunch he played for never seemed to kick off with more than nine.

Going lower down the scale, it's very rare to come across a Subsoccer player who's been injured in the region of the upper thigh. Subsoccermen do, of course, take great care of the Very

Important Pair (remember The Red Sea Syndrome) although I did once spend several days in Charing Cross Hospital after a seven-foot-six American volleyed me instead of the football. No, you need to go to the game's higher levels to find really painful stories in this area. A famous forward of the 1930s and a recent international midfield player both ended up one down in the course of their careers, but I'm sure they took suitable revenge. As the forward said, a man who commits that kind of foul takes quite a lot of forgetting.

I certainly won't forget watching a right back who had a metal kneecap. The day I saw him, four of the opposition were carried off after kicking this violently, and severely damaging their toes.

I have also heard of a goalkeeper who turns out for a South London side in spite of having a wooden leg. In one game, it seems, he accidentally avoided a goal by losing the limb while dashing out to meet an incoming forward. The striker promptly fainted and the keeper crawled far enough to fall on the ball. Faced with this tricky situation – one-legged goalkeeper unable to get up, attacker in deep shock – the subref very sensibly blew for a free kick. He then booked the unconscious forward for taking a dive in the box.

To end this slightly ghoulish series of reminiscences, I suppose I should quote the claim of my actor friend Jim – not the am-dram chap, but a real, live professional actor who actually gets paid for, well, acting. Not surprisingly, he does tend to be a little dramatic, and as soon as he heard about the man with one arm he immediately stated he had once played against a centre half with no head. This, however, is clearly absurd. Obviously he would have been put at full back, to cover his weakness to the high ball. Jim is so unreliable.

A YOUNG TURK

Another team-mate of mine was much more reliable: you could

always count on him to kick anything above ground level until it was level with the ground. What he lacked was the power of speech.

To be fair, he could in fact talk, but simply spoke very little English. The player in question was a young Turk – I use the term literally – called Omar, a pupil of mine at one of those language schools quaintly set among the strip clubs and sauna parlours of Soho. I was teaching there to supplement my meagre student's grant, and when I introduced him to my Sunday side in Richmond he was a great success. Omar turned out to be one of those typical continental defenders, skilful but with a touch of steel. He also called me 'Meester Robbie', which I found quite pleasing.

Unfortunately, as he grew in confidence, he began to commit the kind of atrocities you read about in the rise of the Ottoman Empire. He really did kick very hard indeed. This obviously did our opponents no good at all, and in the end made me very tired as well. As his mentor – some said keeper – I had to trot around the field to the scenes of his assaults to explain and interpret.

'I'm so sorry. He's from Istanbul, you know,' or, 'That's right, Omar. Refereeman say he depart you from pitch,' and so on.

But he got worse. In one match our own manager, a late refereeing stand-in, had to book him after a horrific two-footed tackle that caught someone around the neck. He bowed very neatly and apologetically, the way they all seem to, and then tackled the same player around the head.

And he took to terrifying people verbally, too. Realising they would be unlikely to understand Turkish, he would make strange little grunting sounds as he tracked down his victims. I remember one day in Staines when he chased a little winger all along the half-way line, from one side of the pitch to the other, until the poor man dribbled straight into touch, Omar snorting away behind him.

'Have him off, ref!' he pleaded. 'He's noising me!'

DOCTORS IN TROUBLE

With so many chronic invalids taking to the subfields of the nation, and so many others lying all over them after meeting maniacs like Omar, it's not at all a bad idea to have some form of medical assistance on hand. The easiest way of doing this is to pick a doctor in the side.

When kept under proper control, these people can be quite useful, especially when it comes to getting into hospital bars – which apparently never close – nurses' homes and so on. Their actual medical duties, however, should be confined to very simple tasks, such as deciding whether someone is, say, drunk or sober, awake or asleep, even dead or alive. Doctors should be treated with the utmost suspicion when they try to diagnose injuries on the pitch; they will either announce that a man knocked out after a clash of heads is suffering from some strange, exotic sickness such as beri-beri, or go to the other extreme and insist that someone with a leg broken in five places should stop shamming and run it off. Lifelong cripples can be fashioned in this way.

And another thing. Never allow two doctors to play together in the same team. They will spend whole hours discussing the victim's condition while he slowly succumbs to frostbite on the penalty spot. Also, never, ever trust medical students who are slogging through their teaching hospitals. All their diagnoses are dictated by the particular juicy ailments or bodily functions they're studying at the time. I remember one of my friends up to his neck (almost) in gynaecology who insisted that our sweeper was pregnant.

'But I'm not even married!' he wailed.

Law Thirteen
*Everything and everyone enjoys a visit to a Subsoccer
ground, except, of course, those who have anything at all to
do with the match.*

Other people to be viewed with extreme caution, in spite of their
obviously good intentions, are members of the St John's Ambulance. Most subsoccermen are quite terrified of them, and will
happily bleed to death rather than fall into their clutches. The
result of this is that the ambulancemen get very little to do on a
Saturday afternoon, and are even more keen to do well when
they can get their hands on a patient.

This reminds me of a striker with one of my old teams who
said he had to leave the field because of a calf strain; really,
I think, he went off for a sly smoke – our captain was one of
those hopeless idealists who object to that type of thing on the
pitch. Anyway, somewhere in the pavilion, the St John's boys
pounced. We trooped back to the dressing-room after the match
to find him laid out on a bench, covered from head to foot in
crêpe bandage. We called him the Mummy from then on, and he
never walked properly again, although he naturally continued
to play Subsoccer.

A RESCUE IN ROTHERHAM
Of course, subsoccermen can always try a spot of first aid themselves – by chasing away St John's Ambulancemen, for instance,
as they hover, vulture-like, around helpless team-mates. Some
people claim this is the finest first aid of all, but I can't quite
agree, since my friend Pat once saved a player from drowning on
the pitch.

Almost, anyway. It wasn't exactly on the pitch, but it was
right next to it. Pat was playing somewhere up in the wilds of
Yorkshire – I think it was Rotherham – on a ground where the

We called him the Mummy from then on, and he never walked properly again, although naturally he continued to play Subsoccer.

touchline ran alongside a narrow but loathsome canal. With his team hanging on to the lead and the minutes ticking away, they won a corner; and being a good, plain no-nonsense Yorkshireman, the winger turned and planted this in the middle of the lifeless waterway. One of the other side plunged in to fish it out, and completely disappeared from view. He would have stayed that way, too, but Pat cleverly fished him out with a corner stick. The poor man lay on the bank for the rest of the match, heaving up huge helpings of canal water. Pat said the chap was afraid to smoke for six weeks afterwards in case he set his breath alight.

Obviously, I can't match this sort of lifesaving myself, but I did help staunch severe blood loss for a side that seemed set to lose gallons of the stuff.

I was working in a holiday camp, organising the football matches, and one day every single player representing Woodbines (or whatever their silly team was called) turned up with his neck covered in spectacular bites. Now there are no mosquitoes in Barry Island, and not too many vampires, either, so it didn't take too long to work out what they'd been up to the night before. Luckily, I got hold of just enough elastoplast to go round, so they covered their throats with this and played on, looking like men who'd just escaped from Sweeney Todd. I managed some very interesting chalet numbers out of that one.

ANIMAL MAGIC

I don't suppose a vet would have been much use that morning, but most afternoons a man in his line could have a field day. Animals love Subsoccer, and any submatch anywhere usually attracts more of them than you hope to find in the average zoo. Dogs are very keen, but they do tend to stop watching and start playing instead. I remember a schoolboy cup tie when a very unselfish spaniel totally confused their defenders with a superb dummy run that let our centre forward in for the winner. And my friend Jim claims he once saw an afghan hound score a hat-trick on Hackney marshes, which I almost believe.

Since Subsoccer grounds seem to be found in so many odd, out-of-the-way places, it's very common for other beasts to turn up, too. This is especially so in the Rhondda Valley, where sheep double up as lawn mowers. A side benefit of that is that you can collect enough wool for a decent-sized sweater from the railings around the pitch, but it can sometimes be difficult to persuade the flock to seek pastures new when Saturday comes. A full back in yet another of my old sides always took his mad alsatian, a vicious-looking brute with a taste for lamb chops, to any match north of Taffs Well. All of a sudden the sheep just seemed to leave.

Cows also make good grass cutters, but sometimes spoil everything by the regularity with which they empty their bowels: this, I imagine, must be something to do with having so many stomachs. I can think of a team in Bonvilston, near Cardiff, which boasted a ground record stretching back to the days of Owen Glyndwr simply because of this. Finding space on that pitch had nothing at all to do with tight marking. It wasn't so much a case of avoiding the pats as picking out the drier ones. The home players, of course, seemed to know each of them on a personal basis – 'Nasty one, that, butt. One of Blodwen's. Fresh, eh?'

On a similar note, I once played in a match at Singleton, just outside Preston, on a ground next to a pig farm. I now understand why everyone in football has always assumed the poor animals are sick. I know they made us ill enough. It was one of those days when everyone had a stinker.

STRICTLY FOR THE BIRDS

Birds tend to be a little too small to add to the air of confused chaos in which subgames take place, although my friend Pat once turned out in a match in Leeds that was interrupted by an albatross. Apparently there was a strange, beating noise, and then everything went dark as this great white bird flew across the sun. The game stopped completely as both teams watched it come, pass, and sail slowly into the distance. They then looked at each other, shrugged, and carried on with the kicking.

I can't quite come up with anything to compare with that, but I do remember a canary at Amersham, which hopped around our goalmouth for a good twenty minutes. And I once saw a game in which the left back abandoned all interest in the second half to stalk and finally capture a stray parrot. Oddly enough, and unlike the pigs, this was not sick.

HOME BANKERS

What with all these happy sightseers, it's easy to understand why Law Thirteen informs us that 'Everything and everyone enjoys a visit to a Subsoccer ground, except, of course, those who have anything at all to do with the match'. There is, however, one other type of person whom the players themselves would be delighted to see there.

I have always dreamed of opening the cupboard in the dressing-room (when the dressing-room is actually bigger than the cupboard) and finding a pinstriped bank manager smiling confidentially inside, the way you sometimes see in TV adverts. At the moment, subsoccermen spend their matches fretting anxiously about ending up penniless at the final whistle.

The problem is that most dressing-room doors are quite impossible to lock; this, of course, is where there *is* a door, or even a dressing-room, at all. For this reason, only a fool or a philanthropist leaves any cash inside, so a weird, ritualistic ceremony takes place just before the subteam takes the field. One of them will produce a bag and trudge up and down, mournfully crying, 'Valuables! Valuables!' in the doom-laden tones of the drivers of the old plague wagons. And one by one, as if bringing out their dead, the others will hand over money, wallets, watches, bracelets, bangles, beads, betting slips and so on. Most look so sadly at the articles they drop inside that you might think they never expect to see them again. They do not.

Sometimes the valuables bag is given to the team trainer, who will set it down beside the pitch as he runs the line. He is now quite likely to step on it, crushing everything inside to tiny pieces, or even forget it is there as he racks his brains for ways to deceive the referee.

Sometimes, on the other hand, the valuables bag is given to the goalkeeper, who will put it reverently inside the posts. The thinking behind this is probably that, as a less important member of the defence (see club linesmen, p. 107), it's not quite so vital for him to pay full attention to the game. I do wonder, myself, if this can be right. Certainly I believe that another explanation for all the high scoring in Subsoccer lies in security-conscious keepers going cross-eyed by trying to watch both the bag and the ball at the same time. Still, bad goalkeepers can earn themselves very respectable reputations if they do manage to make a go of their guard duties. Men who happily throw in seven goals a game, say, can even end up with Player of the Year awards if they get through a whole season without losing too much of their team-mates' money.

Even then, veteran subsoccermen, determined to make absolutely certain of getting their own back, take other measures, too – wrapping their various articles in a sock, for instance. By using a carefully cultivated specimen, you can not only frighten off potential thieves, but also pick up bonus quantities of cash into the bargain. I've seen players blankly refuse to touch fairly large rolls of bank notes once they've been in the same bag as one particularly obnoxious sock.

An alternative is to wear a money belt. These can be quite

handy out on the pitch in games played soon after pay-day, lend-
ing a useful amount of weight to a well-timed bodycheck, but
they, too, can be tricky. They always seem incredibly difficult to
put on, and I recall a side that played short three weeks running
because the team capitalist could never fasten his until four-
thirty.

Another word of warning. When collecting the contents of a
valuables bag, be very careful in your choice of words. Do not,
for example, ask anybody to 'Put your valuables in here'. The
response will be obscene, and totally predictable.

A SNAPPER-UP OF NOT INCONSIDERABLE TRIFLES
None of the usual security systems, however, could cope with a
man called Bert who came very, very close to breaking Law Thirteen by having a marvellous time whenever he came to the
ground. Except that it wasn't the match he enjoyed, but what
went on around it.

Bert turned out for one of the better sides I've sometimes
managed to sneak into, one that played in a very fair standard of
football – right on the border, in fact, between the subgame and
the real thing. This, to an extent, was Bert's undoing, and ours,
too. Because we actually changed in proper, lockable dressing-
rooms, we never used a valuables bag at all. After a couple of
Saturdays we started to find money, watches, pens and the like
missing from our pockets, and after a couple more Saturdays
managed to work out that Bert was our man.

He never seemed to lose anything at all – that was the give-
away; and we began to realise that he was always the last out
onto the pitch at half-time, which must have been when he took
his unofficial collection. Soon after that, a refereeing policeman
confirmed our worst fears.

'Oh, Bert!' (The name has of course been changed to protect

the guilty.) 'Oh, Bert!' he chuckled. 'He's a klepto! Thought you knew.'

The trouble was that finding out about Bert didn't really solve anything. We didn't feel we could denounce the man to his face (in any case, he was quite big), but nor could we keep losing money. We did toy with the idea of bringing in a valuables bag, but by then we were convinced that Bert would find some way to steal that as well.

And things got worse. Bert began to take a liking to articles of clothing, too, so we developed the habit of turning up for games in our oldest jumpers and jeans, becoming more and more scruffy until one Old Boys side refused to let us into their club-house at all.

The outlook was bleak, but then, suddenly, Bert disappeared. Apparently someone took a tie-up from his kitbag, and he was so disgusted by this act of appalling dishonesty that he left in a huff. For a while we had no idea where he had gone, but then we saw another team on their way to a match, half in boiler suits, half in pyjamas, and we knew.

Law Fourteen
Anything that might not fit, will not fit.

Bert, of course, suffered from a mental disorder. Come to think of it, we suffered from it, too, possibly more than he did. Most of Subsoccer's villains, however, carry out rather more physical crimes, doing far more damage than they really should because of the pitiful state of their victims. Subsoccermen, being so very slow, are always being kicked, even when nobody means to kick them at all. And being generally old, unfit, and basically brittle, they also get hurt. Shin-pads would help, but since subsoccer-men quite naturally resent paying out anything at all to be humiliated week after week, these feature fairly low on their list of priorities. Even when they do come across a pair – in a Christmas cracker, say – submen are reluctant to wear them.

Unless kept in place with sellotape or sticking plaster, the pads constantly slip round to the wrong side of the leg; and even if they are stuck where they should be, underneath the socks, they cause more pain than they prevent, pulling out a forest of tiny hairs when you try to take them off. This is agony indeed.

I gave a lot of thought to ways of avoiding this, and then came across an old pro (no, not that kind of old pro) called George. Before one game I saw him take two paperbacks out of his kitbag and lay them on the bench. This was odd, since George was the sort who never even reached Page Two in *The Sun*, so I watched carefully as he solemnly bent each book and stuffed it down the backs of his socks.

'Those pads are all right, see, but you get kicked from behind as well, and that's worse,' he explained. 'Lots of the lads used to do this.'

Now a subplayer hardly ever runs past anyone, and so isn't likely to be attacked that way; and, of course, he would never, ever be foolish enough to try to 'shield' the ball. What a target to offer! No, but if the paperbacks are pushed down the *front* of the socks, they do a far, far better job than bona fide shin-pads ever could.

The choice of books, though, is obviously vital. Heavy stuff like *War and Peace* or *Ulysses* wouldn't really do, since most of us simply couldn't shake a leg under the weight of all that literature. Agatha Christie is pretty good, and so is James Hadley Chase; early Len Deightons and John Le Carrés are fine, too, but you need to be fit to take their later stuff. The point is that you can always vary it, depending on the quality of the opposition. For a fairly timid side you might need no more than an E.M. Forster; a tougher bunch might merit a middle-period Graham Greene, or a D.H. Lawrence. Really nasty outfits could drive you to a Brontë, and for thorough-going thugs you might even run to a Dickens. If in doubt, the team could always take on a W.H. Smith's salesgirl, the way golfers hire caddies.

I should add the probably needless advice that such books should always be paperbacks and nothing else. My friend Jim, so often one to carry things to extremes, once tried to turn out in Tooting with the bound editions of *The Pickwick Papers*, Volumes One and Two, down his socks. The referee quite rightly made him remove them, and then went on to take his name when he found they were GLC library books and eight months overdue.

BOOT MONEY

One item of kit that must, unfortunately, be bought is a pair of football boots. Mountaineering boots, wellies, galoshes and even flippers would often be better, but referees probably wouldn't allow them, and in any case they're not made with those nice little stripes down the side. The real thing, though, does seem rather expensive these days, so it's wise to find the cheapest pair around and settle for that. Spending money on anything more sophisticated is a complete waste of time. The average subsoccerman is so unco-ordinated that even the very latest in scientific sportshoes, the ones that really ought to let you overlap on Everest, will do no good at all. Pick something simple, preferably in pretty colours, and think no more about it.

On no account be tempted by the bizarre styles that always seem to appear a couple of weeks before Christmas. I remember a friend who bought a pair just like this, one with a specially-designed revolving stud unit. This was supposed to help you turn on a 20p piece without effort, stress or strain and generally make you play like Maradona. He wore them for the first time on a mudheap somewhere in Mortlake and ended up glued to

the spot near the half-way line, spinning slowly round and
round like a very sad top.

A SHAMEFUL SHOT

Whatever boot you finally choose, it is important to make sure
that it fits, more or less. I still shudder at the memory of one of
the most embarrassing incidents I have ever witnessed in my
entire subcareer, all caused by a pair that didn't. For some
reason my friend Pat has never been able to buy football boots to
match the size of his feet. Perhaps they shrink shyly whenever he
goes into a shop – I do not know. Anyway, the boots always turn
out to be too big, so he ends up stuffing them with newspapers,
socks, carpets, curtains and so on to keep them on at all.

We were playing a representative game for London University
against an FA XI, no less, at Wealdstone's ground in North
London. Unfortunately, quite a few people came along to
watch, including some involved in proper soccer. Late in the
second half, Pat tried a shot, missed the ball, and sent his right
boot flying onto the roof of the stand.

This is honestly true. Gradual hysteria crept around the terraces as spectators began to realise the full absurdity of what
they had seen. Pat raced off the field to find a substitute shoe, terrified, he said later, of being refused his souvenir FA bridge set
for bringing the game into disrepute. Our coach, Eammon
Dunphy, who, I'm sure, will be absolutely delighted to be men-
tioned in this book, had to be restrained from leaving the ground
and possibly even the country. Pat later sneaked out of the after-
match buffet, borrowed a ladder, and retrieved the prodigal
boot.

I suppose I ought to add that in the same game I somehow
managed to let in a 65-yard centre from Cyrille Regis. He has
since gone on to become a real footballer, although perhaps not
on the strength of that goal. On the other hand, that same goal

may well explain why I haven't.

Just one more word of advice. When you buy a pair of boots, do your best not only to try them on but also to count them. I realise this does seem fairly basic, but I have actually seen players come straight from the sportshop to the game, open the box, and find only one boot inside. And just the other week our centre forward spent half an hour trying to force his way into a new pair apparently meant for a man with two right feet. As a man with two left feet, he found them quite useless. Law Fourteen of Subsoccer does insist that 'Anything that might not fit, will not fit', but this sort of thing really can be avoided.

UP AND UNDER

Another significant article of kit is the one you wear under your shorts. Like the riddle of the Scotsman and the kilt, this has become one of the great questions of our time, mainly because no real subsoccerman would ever be seen undressed in a jock-strap, athletic briefs or anything like that. They generally go in for bathing trunks, bermuda shorts, or long johns, although some plump for more exotic creations in silk, leather and even rubber. I've never made a really close study of the subject – I doubt if anyone could, without picking up a rather dodgy reputation – but I'm definitely in favour of individuality. Football has become very uniform, after all, and it's nice to find a touch of flair here and there. As it is, the number of actual jockstraps on view indicates a side's status; the more there are, the better it is.

Transistor radios give the same kind of clue, but in reverse. For the subsoccerman, the really important result on a Saturday isn't achieved by the team he plays for but the team he supports. This is quite understandable. Given his uselessness at the game, he is far more likely to influence a match by shouting at it rather than by being in it; and it's for this reason that you often see a side, having lost to a last-minute own goal, over the proverbial because they've switched on to find Spurs have won away, while another lot, who have just scored seven, are sunk in gloom following another Arsenal defeat. To find out whether you should spend the evening drinking (to celebrate) or drinking (to compensate), the transistor becomes quite indispensable. After seasons of being wrapped in towels, however, the radios tend to develop a blotchy, mis-shapen look. This means that they will be subtrannies for ever more, even when retired from active service.

Nowadays, by the way, some who do hang up their transistors may try to replace them with those personalised stereo sets. These musical headphones should be banned outright by all self-respecting subclubs. Many players will simply forget to take them off and wear them onto the pitch. They will then be found boogeying on the half-way line when they should be coming back to pick up.

Law Fifteen
The ability of any subteam stands in inverse proportion to the brilliance of its colours and the sophistication of its name.

In spite of all this, any subplayer in search of a club isn't forced to go scanning kitbags for tell-tale transistors; nor does he have to creep about changing-rooms, peeping through key-holes to see the same side squeezing themselves into their shorts. In fact, he needn't even watch them play. All that's necessary is to take a quick look at their colours and find out what they're called. He can then simply apply Law Fifteen of Subsoccer.

In this way, Red Star Romford, in their rainbow-striped shirts and satin shorts that make them look like a squad of Pied Pipers, will inevitably be awful. On the other hand, Ironworks FC, with their 1930s-style jerseys that may once have been grey and

Musical headphones should be banned outright by all self-respecting subclubs.

unfashionably-hooped socks, will be the scourge of the local leagues. It all comes down to that compensation impulse, naturally, but I'm certain all this technicolour kit actually makes bad teams even worse. Surely at least some of these lovely-looking sides are even more hopeless than they should be, simply because the players don't want to dirty their charming outfits.

THE LOWER DEPTHS

Law Fifteen is underlined in submatches that aren't supposed to be competitive at all. Instead they are so-called friendlies, fixed up by inadequates so unutterably bad that they're not even good enough for the average subteam. It goes without saying that these games outdo the fiercest cup ties in sheer horror, mainly because the people playing just can't help kicking you.

University throws up several strange examples of this kind (Split Maths v. Microbiologists) as do the teaching hospitals (Osteopaths v. Venereologists), but they certainly don't enjoy a monopoly. Inter-church matches can be every bit as bizarre (Christian Scientists v. Seventh Day Adventists) and every bit as brutal, too.

I once played in a fixture like this out in Slough, a complicated, inter-union affair organised by local journalists and printers. NUJ/NGA v. SOGAT/NATSOPA, I think it was, because I remember the park keeper telling us he couldn't decide whether we were a game or an alphabet. Anyway, our lot were a couple short, so we ended up with one chap who really didn't seem to have played much football at all. He was quite keen but also quite unco-ordinated (he is still the only man I have ever seen kick himself in his own head), and not surprisingly tended to hover on the fringes of the action. Just before the end, though, I accidentally passed to him and then saw, to my relief, that he was standing all alone in about twenty yards of space.

'Time!' I shouted, trying to help. 'Time!'

'Oh, about quarter past twelve, actually,' he said, looking at his watch.

AN HISTORIC EVENT

I still regret missing another awe-inspiring match of this sort, one arranged by a typical 'inadequate so unutterably bad, etc' – my actor friend Jim. To pay his way through drama school, where he handed over vast sums of money for the privilege of pretending to be an orange pip or a winkle, he took a series of incredibly sleazy jobs. Eventually he worked in a sex shop near Victoria Station. This meant that any subteam he played for always turned up late, since everybody would insist on collecting him there and would then find excuses never to leave. But anyway, for some strange reason, Jim finally decided that his drama school and his sex shop ought to get together on the football field.

The sex shop, a little short of staff, was allowed to pick customers, too. Most agreed to play once they were promised that the team wouldn't be printed in the local paper, so Jim turned out for the opposition. He had to. The fact that he knew the shape of a football had already persuaded the other students that he had abandoned all the easy glamour of pro football for art and the stage. Only people who have seen Jim spend whole seasons offside can really appreciate the hilarity of this. Luckily he had to rope in another friend of mine, Phil, a no-nonsense chemistry student with a talent for splitting centre forwards the way other scientists split atoms. If he hadn't been there, Jim would undoubtedly have organised a Watergate-style cover-up of the whole mad event.

Everything was borrowed, of course – kit, ball, posts, pitch, the lot – and the match took place, furtively, in Regent's Park, a sort of elephants' graveyard of doomed, dreadful games. Phil, not usually an emotional man, comes near to tears whenever he tries to describe the general weediness of the actors who lined up alongside him. Two were discovered making each other up in the toilets, four wore tights, and no less than five took the field in tinted glasses. Legend has it that the students played in black lace and gold lamé (they had just done *Cabaret*) while the sex shop wore latex.

Even now, Phil will hardly speak of what happened that day. It seems that the goalkeeper, a Canadian, took quite a fancy to him, and refused to give the ball to anybody else. He would skip up to him, place it at Phil's feet ('YOU have it!') and trip happily away again. The sex shop regulars, lurking and slinking in a way that made them very difficult to mark, soon caught on and began to pile in the goals. They were, said Phil, quite quick without their dirty macs. The final score is officially described in dozens.

This strange conflict between pornography and art had an interesting sequel some months later, when I dragged Phil along to see Jim's end-of-term showcase production. Apparently he didn't realise what he was watching until ten minutes into the first scene. Then he kicked me playfully on the kneecap and said, in a penetrating whisper, 'My God! I have played football with some of these people!'

For the rest of the rather experimental piece, he glared fixedly at the stage, face clenched and mouthing the odd obscenity. I sensibly waited until the final curtain to ask more.

'What were they like?' I said.

'They are a lot better at acting than they were at football,' he announced at last, after a long pause.

'But, Phil, you thought the play was awful,' I went on.

He gazed at me, turned away, and spat, narrowly missing a passing usherette.

A PRIVATE AFFAIR

My favourite story about a game of this kind was told by my friend Nervous Nelson. He was on some sort of weekend course, held in the wilds of Cheshire, and after the usual Saturday night you suffer at these meetings, went for a Sunday morning walk to try to recover. After wandering aimlessly around for a while, he came across a football match. It was going on at a sheltered, almost hidden ground beneath a hill, and he decided to stay and watch.

The game was fairly dismal, and after a while he strolled over to the only other spectator, a rather puzzled-looking chap busily restraining an enthusiastic dalmatian that seemed to want to play on the wing.

'Morning,' said Nelson.

'Morning,' said the man.

'Who's playing?' asked Nelson.

'It's the Knights of St Columba versus the Freemasons,' answered the other man, a little doubtfully.

'What's the score?' said Nelson.

'I don't know. They're keeping it secret.'

4
The Referee

Law Sixteen
*Referees should be seen and not heard, except when
they are not even seen at all.*

So far, this book has advised the hopeful subplayer on finding a
team, finding the ground, and even finding his feet when he gets
there. Please do not tell anyone this, though. Gratitude is all very
well, but I certainly can't take responsibility for anything that
happens once the whistle blows. It's the dreaded man in black
you answer to now, the judge, jury and jester of the subgame's
court – the referee. This isn't easy, but there it is. He exists, and
we must try to understand him, even if he can't always understand himself.

What he does know is that there's one task he must perform as
soon as he turns up for any match; and that is to declare the
pitch playable. This he has to do, even if it seems a better idea to
pick sides for water polo instead. If the game is to be called off, it
will be called off by the groundsman, cancellation of matches
being the sole aim and purpose of these men's lives.

To do this, and so steal a morning or afternoon off, they will
invent a whole series of strange reasons, from weird diseases of
the grass to obscure religious festivals. All groundsmen hate all
referees, seeing them as a threat to their own authority, and so
do their best to sabotage them right at the outset. I now believe
that the only way to make sure a game does go on is somehow to

convince the subref that it shouldn't. The groundsman will then have no alternative but to disagree and insist that the match is played after all. He may even volunteer to referee it himself.

THE NEW APPROACH

Apart from inspections like this, subplayers don't often see their subref before they roll out onto the pitch itself. If the game is on one of those huge recreation parks, where around five hundred matches go on at once, you may watch a whole bunch of officials edge out of the dressing-room at the same time. They then troop off towards their distant bits of field, huddling together for as long as possible, rather like wagon trains creeping through Indian country. This always makes me wonder about the correct collective noun for this group of subrefs – A flock of referees? A fuss? A bustle? A bumble? A jumble of referees? A junta?

Anyway, as the little band trudges off into the unknown, individuals peel off one by one to meet their various victims.

'Hullo? Dynamo Dagenham and Bayern Mortlake? Oh, good...'

Things changed for a while with the idea that a referee should wander round the teams' changing-rooms, checking up on studs and generally getting to know them before everybody went out. That was the theory, at any rate. What really happened was that both sides ignored all efforts to make friends (why pretend?) and also did everything possible to con the poor man about their boots (why not pretend?). This really was ridiculously easy. I once saw one timid chap accidentally inspect our sweeper's studs eleven times over, taking no notice at all of the rest of us, before dashing for the door. And I knew a midfield thug who always made a point of having new boots for every game. Well, almost. It was always the same pair, really. For a whole season he wore them for the referee's stud parade, only to pack them away again before trotting onto the pitch wearing lethal-looking things that were some sort of cross between ice skates and running spikes.

THE GHASTLY GLOVE

Boots were one thing, but referees definitely ought to start to check, or at least try to check, goalkeepers' gloves which, nowadays, can be every bit as dangerous. Most of the massive, gauntlet-like contraptions on the market at the moment may well have been specially designed by centre forwards, since they make it quite impossible to catch the ball. They're very good for catching people's legs, though. All those pimples and suckers can pull very respectable chunks out of socks, shorts, and even skin, so the subref really should take a look.

I once played in a game in Ashford where our keeper was an amiable giant called Alex. His height often helped him to do some bizarre things – I remember him leaping to reach a ball that was going over the bar and brilliantly tipping it down into the net – but it wasn't his size that did the damage that day.

One of their side went dancing through the middle, and Alex lumbered out to meet him, ready for a death-defying dive at the forward's feet. Down he went, oozing slowly across the ground like toothpaste coming out of a tube, and the striker neatly flicked the ball past him. He did not follow it. As Alex grabbed desperately at thin air, those ghastly gloves fastened on the attacker's thigh with a horrible slurping, sucking sound. It was the sort of noise you hear when the Creature From The Black Lagoon wraps its tentacles round its prey. Alex's victim screamed in agony as all those suction pads and pimples clamped themselves to him. He then fainted, and had to be carried from the pitch. At first it seemed as if Alex might have to go with him, his hands still stuck fast to the poor man's legs. He detached himself just in time, but had to abandon his Harold Schumacher specials and borrow some woolly mittens from a passing schoolgirl.

The subref was quite happy about Alex using those, although I can't say the rest of us were. Still, in my time I've seen referees scratching their heads and puzzling over goalkeepers who turned up with all sorts of weird and wonderful wear. These include riding gloves, driving gloves, gardening gloves, policeman's gloves, elbow-length ladies' evening gloves, washing-up gloves, industrial gloves, surgical gloves, batting gloves, wicketkeeper's gloves, a baseball glove (just the one), a golf glove (also single), deep-sea diving gloves and even, once, boxing gloves.

These were worn by a very polite little fellow who told the subref he'd been dropping so many crosses that he'd decided to start punching instead. This chap didn't play after all, as it happened. He put the boxing gloves on before his boots, and then found he couldn't tie up his laces.

WHAT'S IN A NAME?

That particular subkeeper may not have made the game, but we christened him Rocky anyway. And on the subject of names, it's definitely very important, before the kick-off itself, to find out exactly what the referee is called.

This is vital, since it lends that effective little personal touch to the various appeals you will make during the match. 'Our ball, Mr Strictly!' or 'Our ball, Mr Strictly, sir!' sounds so much nicer than a strangled scream of 'Ref!' When he tells you, however, you must be very careful to keep a very straight face. Otherwise you may well burst into fits of helpless laughter.

All subrefs, you see, and indeed many real refs, seem doomed to bear through life names of quite astounding silliness. I've heard of a Fussy, a Bossy, a Tinkler, a Diddler, a Jolly, and even a Bent. I once came across a man called John Nutt who became so ashamed that he changed his name altogether (to Jeff Nutt) and my friend Jim tells me of a Cretin and a Creep. Anyway, it's

wise to accept that most will sound like characters dreamed up
by Dickens on a bad day and to be prepared.

To be fair to referees, there aren't many players in the subgame who can claim to have proper names themselves. I've
known Gumms, Gosses, Mudds, Munns, Piddocks, Pitkins, Ske-
hans, Stoddarts and Shamashes, and the Christian names aren't
much better, either. Every Fred, George, Cecil, Cedric, Silas,
Herbert, Horace and Percy stamped out in decent society seems
to turn up in one subside after another. I wonder, sometimes, if
careless parents don't actually condemn their children to Subsoccer in the cradle itself. Certainly you don't find many an
Andy, Bobby, Dean, Stuart, Shane or Wayne among our lot, the
way you do in all real teams (except Middlesbrough.)

RELATIVE NORMALITY

Silly names or not, I suppose most subrefs are fairly sane when it
comes to their behaviour – especially compared with the players
they try to control. I suppose the law of averages must be responsible for this. Regularly to find twenty-two certifiable lunatics in
6,000 or so square yards is remarkable enough; to find twenty-
three might be pushing things just that little bit too far.

Mind you, there are exceptions. I can think of one rather odd
gentleman who cleared up one of those colour clashes that sometimes come after a mix-up over shirts. He did this by letting both
teams turn out in all-blue. He walked around staring at everyone
for a few minutes before the match and then announced that
everything would be fine.

'Never forget a face,' he told us happily. Unfortunately, since
we'd never seen three of our side before, we did.

I also remember one day when a referee we called Family
Favourites (he did requests) finally cracked. He had to be forc-
ibly restrained from assaulting, perfectly understandably, our
whining, whinging winger who had droned on for ninety min-

utes of constant complaint. Rules and regulations mean that referees dress fairly conservatively, as well, which again eliminates too much eccentricity. I do recall various subrefs wearing tracksuit trousers, sunglasses, woolly hats and black leather gloves (although not all at the same time), but nothing of a truly startling nature.

In fact, the further down the subgame you go, the more immaculately turned out the referee seems to be. This is because, down there in the lower depths, most subrefs are just starting out on the long climb towards proper soccer. Their kit is new, clean, uncreased and unstained by all the mud and blood they'll pick up in the years to come.

In spite of this, I did once see a rather untidy referee, who turned up to take charge of a game in Ealing, in a distinctly odd incident. After half an hour he broke into a brisk trot and his badge fell off. This surprised me, as I'd always assumed the things were made up in a kind of one-piece arrangement with the pocket, but I picked it up anyway.

'I think you dropped this,' I said helpfully, handing him back the badge. 'I hope this doesn't mean you can't referee any more.'

The poor man was so bewildered that we had to convince him it didn't.

AN ABACUS IN ENFIELD

A man who left *us* bewildered, on the other hand, was one of the most bizarre subrefs I've ever come across. He had some sort of numerical fetish, and we later nicknamed him the Abacus.

It was a match played in Enfield, somewhere off the Cambridge Road in North London, to which we turned up, late, with seven men, and inevitably won. I was in goal, and every time I picked up the ball I heard somebody shout, 'One-Two-Three-Four!' as I kicked it towards our forwards. This was quite distracting. I kept slicing it, hooking it, bobbling it along the

One of the most bizarre subrefs I've ever come across. He had
some sort of numerical fetish . . .

ground or belting it straight up in the air as I tried to look round for the phantom counter. In the end, after miskicking so badly that I almost scored a colossally embarrassing own goal, I walked across to the referee.

'Excuse me, ref,' I said (I always believe in being apparently polite to these people, as I shall explain later). 'Excuse me, but some idiot keeps counting in a loud voice, and it's putting me off.'

'I know!' he answered. 'It's me! Wouldn't want to penalise you for four steps! So I'm counting you down! Ha-ha!'

I said nothing. The man was clearly mad. This became even more obvious as the match wore on, and he began to respond to calls for fouls and so on in a very strange way.

'I know, I know, it's a hard game!' he would cry. 'But we're men, lads, and we can take it! Let's see it through together!'

It was like Henry the Fifth before Harfleur. In the end both teams became very embarrassed and mooched about in silence, afraid to utter another word in case it set off yet another outburst. The last I heard, the fellow was on the Football League list, which only goes to show...

A TRAPPIST IN TWICKENHAM

The Abacus proved exactly why we need Law Sixteen of Subsoccer, the one which tells us that 'Referees should be seen and not heard, except when they are not even seen at all', but I also remember another very peculiar subref who took things to the other extreme altogether.

We called him the Trappist Monk, not because he had a funny haircut, or even a funny habit, but because of the way he dealt with dissent, a method which eventually killed all protest stone dead.

Whenever anybody complained about anything, which of course they quite often did, he would immediately stop exactly where he was. He would then stand stock still, gazing off at the far horizon, and hold this pose, staring and silent, while the poor player shouted himself silly about an inch from his ear. In the end frustration, hoarseness and sheer boredom won the day, and he was left in peace.

I must say I can't recommend this approach to up-and-coming subrefs, since it does seem rather a spineless way to win an argument. It also led to rather long stoppages, and even longer games. Towards the end of the match he would even skid to a halt and snap into his trance if a passing player moaned about the weather. Not really the way to make things flow.

Law Seventeen
Each and every club linesman except Sid is so bent that it would be impossible to hang his picture straight on the wall.

While referees often surprise players, my friend Jim – who does seem to find himself at the centre of some very strange happenings – met one man who left him quite astounded. He turned up to play for the reserve team of our own Sunday side, a little nervous since it was his first game for the club. He was more or less ready when the subref walked in, fully clothed and looking – well, looking the way a referee ought to look. Jim, expecting the stud-check, politely lifted his foot and was amazed, as well as unbalanced, when the man grabbed his hand instead.

'Jim! Great! Nice to meet you! Hope you enjoy it! Now look, you play midfield with Big Hughie. We're three short at the moment so we'll go 5–2–1 with an overlapping goalkeeper...'

Jim stood there, astonished, while the referee launched into a full-scale team-talk, ending with an emotional, up-and-at-'em, make-your-mothers-proud appeal that had many of the team in tears. It was only just before the kick-off that someone told Jim that Sid, a qualified subref as well as our own club secretary, was stepping in as a late replacement.

FLAGS AND FLAWS

Sadly for us, Sid's refereeing pedigree actually stopped him being a proper club linesman whenever the man meant to be in the middle did turn up. He had this terrible tendency to be honest and, compared to other sides, we always felt we took the field one short. Elsewhere in Subsoccer, these people simply act as an extra defender; whenever a goal is scored against their side a sort of Pavlovian reaction compels them to jerk their flag into the air to give offside.

They do this every single time. I once saw one man try to disallow a penalty in this way. Other club linesmen have been known to interfere even more directly, knocking balls back on to the pitch and even bodychecking dangerous wingers, although this is a little rarer. Still, as Law Seventeen tells us, 'Each and every club linesman except Sid is so bent that it would be impossible to hang his picture straight on a wall'.

Less incompetent subrefs realise this and tactfully ignore all signals from the touchline. Would they take any notice if the left back started waving at them with a handkerchief? Exactly.

A CORINTHIAN

Even if all sublinesmen cheat, I can remember one who at least cheated fairly. It was during a game against one of those terribly amateur public school old boys sides, a very civilised affair with the scores satisfyingly level (about seven-all), with around a minute to go. The referee then spoiled everything by awarding an absurd penalty for an obstruction that took place about ten yards outside our box.

It was one of the very worst decisions I have ever seen, and not only our lot but theirs, too, surrounded the referee, begging him

to change his mind; the idiot was adamant. Finally, to our surprise, their captain picked up the ball and put it on the spot. He
then sauntered up and tapped it quite deliberately towards the
corner flag.

There was pandemonium, both sides slapping the skipper on
the back, laughing and shouting. I must admit I was one of the
first to grab his hand. This man was clearly a Corinthian. I'd
never met one before, although I'd read about them and seen pic-
tures on funny-smelling cigarette cards. Corinthians, I remem-
bered, would never score from penalties as they refused to
believe anyone would ever be such a cad and a bounder as to
break the laws in the first place. At school, my teachers told me
they had all died out when we lost the Empire. In fact, they told
me they were the reason *why* we lost the Empire. But there he
stood, alive, breathing, and as batty as ever. Not quite as batty,
however, as the referee, who stopped all the celebrations with a
very, very loud blast on his whistle.

'That flouted my authority!' he screamed. 'That was clearly
dissent! I order you to retake the kick in the proper manner!'

The captain squared his shoulders, and then squared his jaw, too.

'I will not,' he announced, in a high, clear voice (in spite of the
squared jaw).

'I am cautioning you for dissent!' yelled the ref. 'Now retake
the kick!'

'I will not.'

'Then I am sending you from the field!'

The captain cast at the subref a glance of withering scorn,
whole generations of privilege blazing in his eyes, a look upon
his face that seemed to say, 'You are a trade unionist.' He turned
on his heel and marched off, head held high. Just before he left
the pitch he called another of his team across.

'Smith Minor,' he told him, 'you will now take the kick. You
will miss.'

So, as his captain strode heroically towards the pavilion, this lesser Smith, a tiny figure no more than six foot five inches in height, stood shivering behind the ball. We all sympathised: what would he do? And in fact we could have been there, waiting and wondering still, if it hadn't been for our linesman. He started fluttering a very grubby rag back and forth in front of his body, the way real linesmen do, and in the end scuttled onto the pitch itself.

'I make that time, referee,' he said helpfully.

'Time to be added on for the taking of a penalty kick,' snapped the subref.

'Ah, for the first kick, yes. But subsequent retakes arising from misconduct on the part of the attacking team now fall outside that provision since FIFA Amendment 47(B). Surely you hadn't forgotten...'

Obviously the poor man had never heard of this, let alone forgotten it. This was hardly surprising, as it had been invented approximately thirty seconds before, but he did his best to salvage something in defeat.

'Forgotten?' he began. 'Forgotten? Of course I haven't forgotten! I ... er ... never intended the kick to be retaken at all! No! Never! I ... er ... I intended to blow for time as the player ran up, simply to underline the crass stupidity of his captain. You have now ruined what would have been a very valuable lesson, and so...'

He blew for time. Needless to say our linesman was, 1) a hero, 2) drunk by five o'clock, and 3) ill for a week, but at least he'd made his mark.

A DAMSEL DISTRESSED

Given the basic dishonesty of most club linesmen, subrefs rarely allow them to make quite such an impact on the game. In fact the only really dramatic, drastic and – this is the point – totally legal intervention I've ever known wasn't made by a linesman at all, but by a lineslady.

Her name was Rosie, the Irish girlfriend of a faded Irish genius called Gus, a sort of George Best of East Sheen who didn't struggle quite so fiercely against the slide into debauchery. We were playing a very useful outfit over in Acton, hanging on to a surprise one-nil lead but taking a real pasting in one of those desperate, Alamo-style last stands. Nervous Nelson, at right back, had tragically forgotten the bag of sweeties he always used to distract lively young wingers, and was being roasted by a thirteen-year-old flier. The equaliser had to come, and in the end it did – although not according to Gus.

'Offside!' he yelled. 'Sure, that was offside! Linesman!'

The linesman, of course, was Rosie, who was in fact a little bit unlucky to be out there on the touchline and not doing a holding job in midfield. (We really weren't very strong at the time.)

'Offside!' shouted Gus again. 'Offside!'

'Pet, it was not offside,' said Rosie.

'Sure, yer joking, woman!' cried Gus. 'Offside! Get yer flag up! Offside!'

'Pet, it was not offside,' said Rosie again. 'Yer man who put it in was level with yer Nervous Nelson.'

This excited the subref, who had been watching all this with the usual indifference.

'What was that?' he said quickly. 'What? Level, you say?'

'Sure, that's right,' said Rosie. 'Yer man wasn't offside because he was level. Yer Nervous Nelson was...'

'But ... but are you sure?' he went on.

'Sure, I'm sure. Yer man was...'

'But ... but that's offside! Level IS offside! That's the right decision! You're wrong, but you've given the right decision! Offside! No goal! A free kick for offside!'

The referee was ecstatic. He told us later it was the first time he'd ever been able to trust a linesman in twenty-five years in the middle. And the other lot didn't argue too much, either.

'Nobody could be daft enough to pull that one on purpose,' said their centre forward, looking across at Rosie.

'Huh,' said Gus.

SUBTHUG v. SUB JUDICE

Because of this dismal and quite deserved reputation, it's not only referees who often feel sublinesmen really could improve. Players think the same, and sometimes try to persuade the man with the flag to do better – by taking him gently by the neck and dragging him off for, say, a friendly chat. This means that your average linesman does need some sort of protection, and I've generally found this can be quite neatly done by threatening legal action.

Most subthugs go in morbid fear of this, since it could end in payment of fines, something no self-respecting villain can bear. It's wise to do this, however, in a casual, off-hand way that convinces people that this type of thing is all in a day's work: 'Excuse me, Tom, just come over here, will you? This chappie says he's going to rip our linesman's ears off, and I'd like you to take notes for prosecuting counsel.'

This usually persuades would-be ear-rippers, etc., to go away, but to be fair, it can back-fire. I remember one match down by the Thames in Laleham when an especially nasty character indicated to our man on the touchline that he wasn't entirely happy with some of his decisions. He did this by breaking his glasses. Fearing a bloodbath, which might even involve me, I intervened.

'I shouldn't do that,' I said, carefully pushing the useful Tom towards the nasty person. 'This man is a solicitor.'

It didn't work.

'Oh yeah! And I'm a —————— choo-choo train! So!'

We put that one down to experience. Along with the linesman's glasses.

THE LINESMAN STRIKES BACK

Nevertheless, the violence isn't always one-way. It will be some
time before I forget one particular man who made a real impression on me when he took matters into his own hands.

I was playing in that Sunday side in Richmond, the one Jim
somehow joined, and our opponents were a crowd who worked
the South Eastern fairgrounds. They were without doubt the
dirtiest, filthiest, most brutal bunch of subplayers I've ever come
across. Two of them had been sent off by half time, and during the
break several marched over to complain about our midfield playmaker feigning injury. (In fact he was still unconscious.) We all
clustered around the team bucket like the Seventh Cavalry standing around Custer at Little Big Horn, until the game began again.

A few minutes later my friend Pat submerged under a sort of
scrum near the touchline. I strolled over (it never does to arrive
too quickly) and suggested to somebody on the fringes of all this
that while seven onto one was fair enough by me, couldn't we
talk this out sensibly? There was a tap on my shoulder and I
turned to see their chief thug waiting a little too close behind me.
He was a huge, horrible figure who'd been sent off after about
thirty seconds, but here he was again. His name (approximately)
was Ugh, and in a split second I thought, This man is going to
punch me in the face. Then he punched me in the face.

To my surprise it didn't hurt all that much, but I sat down
anyway, hoping he'd go away and punch somebody else. He did.
As I gazed about me, contemplating man's inhumanity to man
and Ugh's inhumanity to me, I looked up to see their linesman
looking down. I shrugged.

'Did you see that,' I asked sadly.

'Yeah,' he said. 'Want to get up?'

'I suppose I ought to,' I sighed.

'If you ――― do, I'll ――― break your ――― nose, you――――.
Stay ――― there!'

So I did, while he reached across and started to throttle our skipper. To be fair, the referee did apologise when I finally rose, warily, to my feet.

'I'm sorry about that,' he said, 'but I've already sent Ugh off once, and I can't go and lock him in the dressing-room. What can I do?'

I sympathised. I doubted whether you could lock the man in the Grand Canyon, let alone a dressing-room, but I did ask about the linesman.

'Just don't talk to me about him!' said the ref. 'You should see what he's been doing with my flag!'

The awful Ugh, by the way, later hit Pat in the teeth when he tried to shake hands after the match. He was banned *sine die* for the sixth time, and actually missed about three games before he brazenly began playing all over again. Funnily enough, we had some decent fixtures against the fairground club after that; they seemed to look on us as friendly rivals, and often joked about that one terrifying meeting. We continued to hate them, but pretended to be nice anyway. Nobody ever lost anything by crawling.

Law Eighteen
Foul play is quite acceptable, but foul language is a capital offence.

It should really be the referee's task, of course, to check the mad violence that's so much a part of our game. Much of the brutality is accidental – once a subsoccerman decides to kick the ball, he often can't help kicking everything else as well. Just as much, however, is the result of sadistic spite. Exactly why so many people who are perfectly nice for the rest of the time spend their weekends doing their best to maul and maim I do not know, but there it is. And the man stuck out there in the middle of all this mayhem has to protect everyone out there from – well, from everyone else.

One of the subref's main problems in doing this is the non-finality of his final solution, the sending off. The trouble with Subsoccer is that players who are sent off often refuse to stay sent off. Like Macbeth's victims – and indeed like the awful Ugh – they keep coming back, sometimes to take revenge. Usually they stand on the touchline and shout obscenities, but they have been known to return to the pitch itself. I once saw one exile put on his toupee and try to sneak back as a substitute – he was a little bald. He almost made it, and indeed, particularly confused subrefs can sometimes be persuaded to allow men who have been given their marching orders to be 'legally' replaced by Number Twelves. Still, they do need to be very confused at the time.

BUNKERED

Then again, subrefs generally are confused, often due to their mad insistence on their dignity. They have to insist on it, because if they didn't, nobody would guess they ever had it.

I remember one example of this crazy obsession in a pre-season friendly up in Blackpool, when the referee brilliantly picked up our right back for a very marginal handling offence. (He caught the ball.) That was fine. Unfortunately, when the player taking the kick placed the ball on the spot, he found a fair-sized hole a good four inches deep. Naturally, he moved it backwards. The referee moved it forwards, back into the hole. The kicker moved it again. So did the referee. And so on. This continued for several minutes until the subref threatened to book the poor man if he didn't take the kick at once.

By this time there was a very decent pit where the spot should have been, and he would have needed a foot shaped like a sand-wedge to dig the ball out at all. He tried, stubbed his toe quite spectacularly, and was carried off. The other lot lost three more in the same way before the fifth man ended the farce by bobbling the ball straight at our keeper. He was so surprised that he actually forgot to dive out of the way and so pulled off the one and only penalty save of his entire life.

GOING OVER THE TOP

The game's traditions, of course, almost demand that players do their best to deceive referees like this. And conning the subref is basically accomplished in the very simplest of ways – by stealing a free-kick, for example, through feigning injury after a tackle. When attempting the possum gambit, as it is known, it's very important to remember the audience you're playing to, and act accordingly. Literally. The poor ref is far more likely to be taken in by wildly-exaggerated displays of distress, with lots of writhing and groaning, than by the delicately understated study of stoical resistance to unendurable agony. So do it big, ham it up, go right over the top and leave nothing to chance.

This is also true of the dive that gets you to the ground in the first place. Give it all you've got, adding, if you can, the double-somersault with half-twist in mid-air, and he may even clap as he blows for the foul.

The only exception to this rule is, of course, my actor-friend Jim, whose theatrical skills must put him in a class all his own. When touched or even breathed on he will collapse in an untidy heap and lie completely still, eyes tightly closed, as if dead. Sometimes it even fools me. There are drawbacks, naturally. I recall one wet and foggy day when he lay, like a corpse, for a good twenty minutes on the far touchline. When we finally re-alised where he was and helped him to his feet, he had to leave the field with influenza.

STICKS AND STONES

Unfortunately, it's a sad fact of Subsoccer that players usually need to do their Old Vic bit to earn any form of free kick at all. Subrefs are always amazingly hot on any sort of dissent; but they tend not to be quite so severe when it comes to more robust deeds of wrongdoing. Bloodcurdling crimes and all kinds of car-nage can go on without check, right under their noses, but they all seem able to pick up and punish a naughty word at distances of one hundred yards and more. I know Law Eighteen explains that 'Foul play is quite acceptable, but foul language is a capital offence,' but I'm still not sure if this is the way it should be. I've never seen anyone taken to hospital after being sworn at, but many of my friends have made the trip to the local casualty wards following more physical assaults.

Once again, it's all down to compensation. Just as the sub-player desperately hopes to disguise the shortcomings that mean he can't play the real game, so the subref frantically tries to win the dignity and respect he never enjoys in real life. Anyway, to be really nasty to them without giving them any excuse for revenge does take a fair bit of skill and effort.

You need both those qualities, too, once you accept that the subref doesn't often protect the more peaceful subplayer. This means he must learn to protect himself. Cowardice helps; so do speed off the mark and a talent for the high jump. Lack of ability can be a bonus, but with Subsoccer standards already as poor as they are, it's difficult to imagine anyone who's simply too bad to be worth kicking at all.

In the end, I suppose the threat of some sort of retaliation is the only true deterrent, but I should stress that the deterrent must be real. Tell the seven-foot-four-inch Neandertal at centre half that if he kicks you just five more times he'll be in big trouble and he may possibly be carried off in hysterics. He may also see to it that you are carried off in very tiny pieces. No, use your wits instead. Don't worry that you simply don't look strong, but make him worry that he might look stupid.

RHETORIC CAN DAMAGE YOUR HEALTH

Our Sunday side in Richmond specialised in this, simply because we had to. We had a fair sprinkling of students in the team at the time, none of them too keen on brain damage with Finals just a few months away. This explained what we called our discretion, but it often seemed to send other clubs into a kind of frenzy, most upset by what they saw, quite correctly, as our cowardly refusal to retaliate. I have to admit we did play this up a little, since it seemed to endear us to referees, and we also took to offering what we meant to be further evidence of our education and general good breeding.

I remember Pat scoring against a fairly homicidal bunch and driving them totally scatty by standing there, gazing at the ball in the net.

'An unpretentious little goal,' he mused. 'Hardly spectacular, but undeniably satisfying.'

After that we sat down and gave some very serious thought to our plan to entertain, instruct and stay alive. For a while it seemed to work.

'Book this man, ref, he's a pragmatist!' became a pretty familiar request. So did, 'Look out, sir, that sweeper's using sarcasm again!' I can think of another game when the other lot's captain piped up with, 'Come on, lads! Let's go forward with the ball and with conviction!' and I demanded whether he was allowed this flagrant use of zeugma in the penalty box.

In the end, though, the whole thing got out of hand. We were so busy dreaming up complaints like, 'Clamp down on that alliteration, ref!' or 'For God's sake, sir, have a look at his hyperbole!' that we began to lose our grip on the game altogether. Most of the side gave it up when a visiting full back flattened our winger with a truly dreadful challenge and then got himself off Scot-free.

'Sorry ref,' he said. 'I'm a logical positivist.'

It had gone far enough.

THE BARD BARRED

I must confess that I did carry this on a little longer, until a very nasty experience in a Spartan League game persuaded me to stop as well. It was another argument – discussion, I would have called it – over that strange four-step rule. I mean to say, what *is* a step? How far do you have to move your foot for it to *be* a step? If your toe trembles, is *that* a step? Anyway, this particular subref penalised me, without a word of warning, very early in the game, and gave a free kick which we somehow cleared. A little later, as he stood near the goal during a stoppage in play, I asked him about it.

'Excuse me, referee. I just wondered if you could explain that last...'

'Four-steps,' he snapped. 'Four allowed. You took five. Indirect free kick. End of matter.' I should have been warned, but I wasn't.

'Yes, I see, ref, but surely...'

'Four steps. No more,' he grated. 'Rules of the game. Four-step law.'

'But surely, referee, that is a law "more honoured in the breach than the observance",' I tripped out merrily.

'That is dissent.'

'Actually, it's Shakespeare,' I told him.

'Sorry, ref,' he said. 'I'm a logical positivist.'

The man was clearly a philistine. He came and stood about an inch from my nose.

'That is dissent,' he repeated. 'This is a book. This is a pencil. This is your last warning.'

I shut up.

Law Nineteen
The only good referee is a bad referee.

Sympathetic Subsoccer referees – and they do exist – tend to take a far more flexible view of the Laws. Enlightened officials, for instance, have no silly ideas about the time they're supposed to allow teams actually to play. They treat the prescribed ninety minutes merely as what the advertising people call a notional norm, sometimes lengthening the match, sometimes shortening it, according to the way things go.

I must say I'm all in favour of this. If everyone's enjoying themselves, why stop? And if they're not, why go on? It's so much more sensible than all that nonsense about a semi-Biblical span of four-score minutes and ten. I myself once refereed a game between a Cardiff Jewish club and a side made up of assorted Welsh gentiles which lasted about two and a half hours, simply because I felt we were all having such a nice afternoon. Needless to say, I finally allowed enough time for the match to end in a draw, the only fair result in such a case. I think it was about fifteen-all by the time we finished, as there were a lot of very bad jokes about tennis.

In the same way, a team of mine taking some terrible stick near South London's Purley Way on one of the wettest days in the history of the world (our right winger claimed he'd been overtaken by a trout), owed a lot to a compassionate subref. He stopped the second half after no more than twenty-five minutes to prevent us from taking further punishment. And the other lot didn't complain, either; they knew quite well that they might need that whistle of mercy in the not-too-distant future.

I do realise, of course, that this type of refereeing would not find much favour at the game's higher levels. Administrators of real soccer, and even of Subsoccer, would certainly frown on it and call it downright wrong. But the players appreciate it, and the feelings behind it. Why, it's even possible that a subref who behaves in this way has actually played the game himself! This naturally means that most of his refereeing colleagues feel he's quite useless, and it also explains Law Nineteen.

A DIPLOMAT AND A DONKEY

This Law would certainly apply to a man I once met who protected not only players, but managers, too. This is important, since any spectators who may accidentally chance to be around can sometimes make things tough for the poor team supremo. At times, he can even be threatened by men in the opposing team.

This happened to Jeff, the manager of that Richmond Sunday club, whose flamboyant outbursts in the local Press had led to a reputation as the Brian Clough/Lord Haw-Haw of West Middlesex soccer. In one game he quite annoyed their left back by telling our right winger that the other chap was a donkey, a mental subnormal, and a sexual do-it-yourself man. In the end the so-called donkey, etc., became rather piqued and promised to help Jeff shuffle off his mortal coil after the match. At this point the subref defused what could have turned out to be a very difficult situation. He very sensibly suggested that Jeff should leave.

With five minutes to go – and, to be fair, the game lost – the subcoach looked at his watch, turned, and marched quickly to his car. He locked himself in this and sat inside for half an hour. The defender jumped up and down on the bonnet a few times, but then gave the whole thing up and went to the pub.

The defender jumped up and down on the bonnet a few times.

AN ORANGE ORDER

Sadly enough, even the club officials who so often benefit by such fine, sensitive, cowardly refereeing tend to show very little gratitude. I remember one of my teams that found itself in serious financial difficulties. (We were broke.) In this severe cash flow crisis we chose as our treasurer a man who would have made Ebeneezer Scrooge seem madly generous. One of his first economy measures was to cut out the subref's half-time slice of orange.

He calculated that in this way, over a season, no less than 3.75 oranges could be saved. This would, he said, transform us from a bankrupt lame duck to an irresistible blue chip investment. At a stroke, he promised; or rather, at a slice.

Our committee considered, and with stunning perception proposed to our annual general meeting two separate motions: 1) That the referee should be provided with his orange, and 2) That the referee should not be provided with his orange. The debate split the club, with some players threatening to burn their own oranges if the subref couldn't have his. In the end the despicable treasurer solved the whole problem by disappearing, taking what was left of our funds with him. It seems he fled to the Isle of Wight. Besides being dishonest, he also had very little imagination.

A FINE MESS

Even a good (i.e. bad) subref would have been forced to report that kind of conduct, I suppose, but I'm glad to say he'd be much more lenient with most of the average subclub's misdemeanours. Nowadays, these can be set out in all their gory detail on the matchcard.

This document, signed by the referee, is now meant to reveal to anyone who cares to read it just how dramatically incompetent you and your team have been on any particular day. Besides naming your players – or at least, naming the men who you're claiming are your players (see The Ringer, p. 159) it supplies a check-list of all-round inefficiency as well. This will tell the League officials about the kick-off time (late; very late; never) about the linesman (very bent; fairly bent; no more bent than you expect) about the goal-nets (bad; very bad; not there) about the corner flags (one missing; two missing; three missing; all missing) and so on. The League officials can then sit down and fine you for everything that isn't as it should be.

Understanding subrefs are vital here. Without a little give and take on their part, subplayers become quite unhinged by this question of fines and how to avoid them. This is probably because they quite rightly resent handing over money to any organisation that pretends it can run their game. Still, avoiding these penalties does sometimes produce scenes of wild celebration. I've seen teams who've just been beaten twelve-nil go quite mad with joy because they've somehow managed to do everything the way the League wants it done.

I can't say this happens very often, though. A couple of seasons ago, in fact, my own Sunday side were having a particularly bad run, turning up later and later each week with fewer and fewer men. This sparked off the usual punishment, and in the end we were even being fined for being fined, paying out amazing sums of money for the privilege of being hammered out of sight. Finally, our secretary wrote a letter to the authorities, pointing out that at a time of economic recession, with companies everywhere feeling the fiscal pinch, it seemed strange that the League had made a profit which was proportionately greater than the one returned by ICI. This, however, did not impress the management committee. They fined us again.

Law Twenty
All submatches are refereed by everyone on the pitch with the exception of the referee.

No matter how sympathetic a subref may be to the problems of the average subclub, he soon comes to realise that everyone's out to cheat him anyway. And it's not only the players who try to deceive him. He also has problems with the ball.

Whenever this disappears into rivers, bogs, sewers, forests, cemeteries and so on, he must make absolutely sure that it does eventually return to the pitch. This can lead to rather prolonged games, with matches sometimes finishing in total darkness, but there really is no alternative. Any substitute ball offered by the other side, you see, will be bound to be part of some low, mean scheme to steal an unfair advantage. This never varies.

I remember a cup tie somewhere in the wilds of the Rhondda when we kicked off facing a howling gale that whipped along the valley. For the first forty-five minutes our poor goalkeeper was peppered with shots, the very latest version of the water-proof, wind-assisting white footballs everyone uses nowadays pinging crazily about our area. It was one of those afternoons when goalkicks double back treacherously and whizz over your own crossbar. Anyway, we turned round only four down, fairly confident of pulling at least a couple back before the end.

Straight from the restart, their right winger walloped the ball over the touchline, off the pitch, over the fence, out of the ground and about two miles down the road towards Ponty-pridd. We never saw it again. The rest of the match was played with a hopelessly heavy sludgy-brown pumpkin which simply wouldn't go more than five yards in any direction, hurricane or not. The score stayed at four-nil.

NETS THAT DON'T

Generally speaking, nobody tries to interfere with the goalposts – although I did see a centre forward's son work wonders with a very flexible set at Richmond's Old Deer Park. His father got five that day, but in the record book they put three of them down to the boy. I do believe, myself, that this sort of rule (and upright) bending should be discouraged, since goalposts cause quite enough arguments as it is. The subnets that hang from them are deliberately designed to let the ball pass straight through, although they are quite splendid when it comes to snaring wandering dogs, children and little old ladies. This can sometimes make it quite difficult to decide if somebody has actually scored. I once saw a four-four draw in Streatham in which no goals really went in at all. By the end of the game the poor subref was holding a referendum every time anyone took a shot.

It was a minor disagreement (i.e. a fight) over one of these semi-goals that caused a very amusing incident in a match between a team of journalists and a side raised by the local branch of the South Wales Constabulary. Things got rather heated and, in the end, one of ours and one of theirs staged a sort of all-in waltz on the halfway line. Harsh words were exchanged.

'You're much too stupid to be a policeman!' shouted the reporter.

'No I'm not!' shouted the officer.

Well, there you are.

DECK OF CARDS

I suppose a pair of binoculars could help the subref in disputes of this type, but then again, the man does have enough to carry already. All those watches, whistles, pens, pencils and notebooks – I often wonder how he moves at all. Sometimes I feel like breaking into applause whenever he breaks into a trot.

In addition to all this, the referee also has to stuff his pockets with other assorted articles – road maps of the surrounding area, for instance, so vital for the speedy post-match getaway. And don't forget the valuables, either. Subrefs have to hump these about as well, since they can't trust anyone else to guard them. Perhaps they should be issued with special valuables bags of their own, embossed with the FA crest, which would be worn slung from the shoulder. These could then be used to chastise offenders – 'Never mind sending him off, ref! Hit him with your handbag!'

The whole load has been increased by the arrival of the red and yellow card system, which seems to have died out in the Football League but is carrying on as crazily as ever in Subsoccer. This, I feel, is a huge insult to subplayers everywhere. After all, any idiot knows when he's being booked without being made to watch the referee stand there changing colours like a sort of footballing traffic light. And it causes quite amazing confusion, too.

I've seen subrefs pull an astonishing collection of objects from their pockets, seen players waved at with cheque cards, blood transfusion cards, birthday cards, driving, television and dog licences and even, once, a passport. In another game, our centre half stood patiently in front of the referee, waiting to be cautioned, while the official ran through a vast range of documents before coming up with a credit card.

'American Express? That'll do nicely,' he told him, giving his name.

In fact, even when subrefs do find the cards they really need, they have a terrible tendency to show you the wrong one, or indeed to show you one when they don't mean to show you anything at all. I remember one jovial fool, nicknamed FA Cup because of his rather distinctive ears, who just couldn't keep the dreaded red rectangle out of his hand. He seemed to be able to produce it from thin air, the way magicians produce pigeons. He

*Our centre forward stood patiently in front of the referee,
waiting to be cautioned . . .*

even brought it out when he wanted a handkerchief to blow his nose; every time he did so he smiled happily and chuckled, 'Oops!'

A NARROW SQUEAK AT SANDHURST

One of the major problems with subrefs, then, is that you never really know just how they will react to anything. This was underlined on a potentially disastrous day in Camberley, during a game against a Sandhurst officer side. They had cleverly taken us to the mess before the match, and in the second half the cold, misty weather began to take its toll on my bladder. I stood there in goal, watching the events at the far end and going through all kinds of agony until I simply couldn't stand it any longer. To my shame I gave up the struggle and turned behind a post for relief, hoping the falling fog would hide me. A little later the referee called me upfield.

'I saw that, you know,' he said, pleasantly enough. 'And I should be very careful.'

'Sorry, ref,' I began. 'With all the mist and so on I didn't think...'

'Oh, you needn't bother about me,' he said. 'It's the house behind your goal that concerns me. Can you see it?'

I looked at the handsome building just thirty yards away. It seemed empty enough, but then I saw a policeman stroll across in front of the windows.

'Princess Anne lives in that house,' he explained. 'I would say you have just been guilty of treasonable exposure. Luckily for you, I am an ardent republican...'

Not only did he let me off with a short lecture, but he also failed to send me to the Tower. For that I shall be forever grateful. Once upon a time they cut off your head for crimes as serious as that. I dread to think what they would have cut off for what I did.

I was very lucky there, but one of the subref's royalist colleagues, or even the same man in a patriotic mood (on the Queen's birthday, say) could have had me hung, drawn and quartered on the halfway line. Because of this inconsistency, the games that go on all around the poor subrefs reach something like a conclusion in spite of rather than because of them. As Law Twenty of Subsoccer so truly tells us, 'All submatches are refereed by everyone on the pitch with the exception of the referee.'

In the end, though, what can you expect? As a final word more or less in their defence, I would add that subrefs are not quite as bad as people say. Mind you, people do say that they are very, very bad.

5
The Rest

Law Twenty-one
Not everyone likes watching soccer, but anybody
watching Subsoccer likes it even less than anyone else.

However incompetent subrefs may be, many would say that the subgame treats them rather shabbily. This may be so, but then it treats everyone shabbily, especially those who turn up to watch it. In fairness, I suppose you can hardly complain about this cavalier indifference to spectators, since there tend not to be many of them.

There are many obvious reasons for this, but I still believe it's all terribly sad. One of the lesser known facts about the great French writer Albert Camus, for instance, is that he actually played in goal for a pro side in Algeria. All that he knew about men, he once admitted, he had learned through football. Now I would never try to claim that the average subplayer will develop, say, a healthily optimistic existentialism through suffering Subsoccer: he is far more likely to develop into a gibbering wreck. Even so, there's definitely a lot to be discovered about your fellow humanity by casual observation. The public, I feel, really ought to know.

By the public, I mean that great mass of untold millions who are not and have never been subplayers, subcoaches, submanagers or subrefs — or at least, not intentionally. One of the

131

great problems of being subspectators, you see, is that it is so very difficult to stay that way.

The problems begin if they arrive in time for the kick-off itself, which is likely to mean that they will end up not watching, but playing. So many of the subplayers themselves turn up consistently late that a regular fan can find himself an ever-present player in the team he's supposed to be supporting. People who prefer to drop in on different sides every week, on the other hand, tend to set weird records by appearing for a huge number of clubs every season. This can lead to very strange discussions with friends.

'Thought you gave up after the operation,' they will say. 'Who do you play for now, then?'

'Oh, anybody.'

This usually stops the conversation stone dead. Every so often, however, somebody will want to know more.

'All right, then. Who did you play for last week?'

There will be a longish pause before the answer.

'Can't remember.'

The marvellous oddity about this custom of completing teams by press-ganging any stray civilian within reach is that both sides are always happy to see it happen. Amazingly enough, even clubs that do somehow manage to turn up with eleven men will move heaven and earth to persuade passers-by to play for the struggling opposition. This may sound ridiculous, since they will do their best to kick as many of the other lot as possible off the pitch as soon as the game begins, but it isn't quite as absurd as you might think. All subplayers hate *starting* against depleted teams because, remember, these inevitably beat them. Also, to take on six men and a confused jogger, for example, does reduce things to a totally laughable level. All subgames are laughable anyway, if we're being honest, but subplayers prefer to preserve every possible illusion.

A FAMILY AFFAIR

Even when spectators escape being dragged into action, they're
likely to find themselves in the thick of things – not by playing,
but by refereeing. The occasional subref can sometimes forget
that it's not his job to call games off (think back to the groundsman) and refuse to start. Others may be unable to start simply
because they haven't turned up. This always disgusts subteams
who hang around waiting for them, but given all they suffer
when they do come, I tend to find it far more surprising when
they get there at all. In any event, it's at times like these that the
faithful spectator once more steps in to fill the gap.

I remember a rather murky Sunday morning near Heathrow
when one subref left us in the lurch by coming along and then,
very strangely, going away again. When he did eventually show
his face, the fog was clearing by the minute, and by kick-off time
the whole pitch was clear, except for the odd wraith of mist that
swirled playfully around our knees. Everyone knew the game
would go on. Everyone that is, except the referee.

Somehow his heart just wasn't in it – the team voyeur talked
about a spectacular blonde seen sitting in his car – and he
claimed the visibility was just too poor. We disagreed. He insisted. We disagreed again. Finally he marched to the centre
circle, stood on the halfway line, and looked around him.

'From where I stand now,' he announced, 'I cannot even see
the corner flags.'

'But referee,' said our skipper, 'there are no corner flags.
Somebody stole them last month.'

'Irrelevant,' he went on. 'I see no corner flags, and so the
match is off.'

This broke every law in the subgame book, and possibly even
a few in the real game's as well, but we seemed to be stuck. Luckily, and as so often happens, a spectator came to the rescue,

kindly volunteered by one of their lot who sidled furtively into our changing-room.

'Er, listen,' he said, 'my Dad could do it. He's supposed to be our linesman, but my Mum's come, too, so she could do that instead...'

So that was that. As we all know, sublinesmen are without doubt the most dishonest race of creatures on the face of the earth, but for some unfathomable reason they become paragons of justice if they have to referee instead. Nobody can really explain this. Perhaps it's just too easy to cheat when you're handed absolute power, and it becomes an even more enormous challenge to be fair. Anyway, this chap did remarkably well. He even started to ignore his wife out on the line once he realised she was waving to say hello. But then, just before the end, he blew up when his son savagely volleyed our centre forward a good thirty yards into touch.

'I'm not going to send you off for that,' said his father. 'But when I get you home I'm going to give you a damn' good hiding!'

It was too much for the lad, and he snapped.

'He's picking on me again, Mum!' he wailed, looking across to her for help. He got it, too. The linesman threw down her flag and stamped her foot.

'Harry, you leave the boy alone!' she yelled. 'It's the same at the house, always on at him! You never give him a chance, do you?'

It all seemed set for a full-scale family row and we stood around squirming with embarrassment. Everyone was terribly relieved when, a couple of minutes later, the game ended, even though we were only one down and pushing for the equaliser. When we last saw them, the linesman was hitting the referee with her hairbrush.

A SHATTERED ILLUSION

I do hope, by now, that all would-be subwatchers know exactly where, or rather when they stand. Just as no players should ever reach a meeting place too early, or in other words on time, so spectators ought to make sure they arrive those vital few minutes late. Even if they're not actually forced to play or to referee, they still run serious risks of another sort.

I shall never forget the look of sheer horror on the face of a nice little girl who, very strangely, took to supporting one of my old teams. She turned up tragically early for a big cup tie to see her idol, our silkily-skilled and top-scoring centre forward, throwing up in the car park. (He had come straight from an all-night party.) The nice little girl never asked for his autograph again, but moped over the eighteen she already had. She switched her admiration, on the spot, to our macho midfield thug; he vomited at full time – along with our sweeper, who completed a rather natty hat-trick – but did so more privately, in the showers, and the nice little girl never knew.

A PHLEGMATIC FAN

Oddly enough, and in spite of the occasionally stunning pre-match shock, subspectators show a lot more resistance when it comes to the nasty surprises that so often occur during the game itself. By then they are well into their stride as sporting ghouls, wallowing in the pitiful distress of others, which is, after all, what they've turned up to see. I'm convinced that all subfans spend the summer trooping around the scenes of natural disasters and horrible accidents, desperate for something to gloat at. All this second-hand exposure to calamity does, however, lead to a calm, resigned acceptance of misfortune – so long as it's other people's misfortune, naturally.

Sometimes this extends to a maddening smugness that nothing whatever can shake. I remember one old codger who used to spend Saturday afternoons at Cardiff's Sevenoaks Park, purely for the purpose of proving he could never be surprised by anything at all. Everything that happened out there on the pitch – a winger sinking on the halfway line; a full back crossing the halfway line – he had seen before. Everything he was told – Cardiff City scoring six in a game; Swansea City scoring six in a season – he had heard before.

'Nothing surprises me,' he would mutter, shaking his head, and the cloth-cap that was always on top of it. Then, one weekend, he wasn't there. A few days later we were a little taken aback when we learned why. A boat had collided with his bungalow. This was even stranger than it sounds (and it sounds strange enough), as he lived a good ten miles from the coast. Apparently it fell off a trailer. We all wondered what he might have said when this ship suddenly appeared in his living-room. He would never tell us. He never did tell us what he felt about Law Twenty-one, either, which told us (and him) that 'Not everyone likes watching soccer, but anybody watching Subsoccer likes it even less than anyone else.' Of course, he really didn't need to.

THE GOAL-GLUT FALLACY

People like that old codger show just why subplayers themselves develop a rather ambivalent attitude to subspectators. On the one hand we're pleased, grateful and – let's be frank – amazed that anyone takes the trouble to come and watch us at all. But on the other we tend to feel that, having taken that trouble, everyone watching really ought to appreciate the spectacle we so selflessly provide. As this book so neatly proves, all human and most subhuman life is there, so the entertainment value is quite enormous. Why, you don't even need goals!

In fact, you're much better off without them. As any self-respecting subsoccerman will tell you, the very best matches

always end in nil-nil draws, while games that finish up eight-all
or whatever are shocking bores. When all's said and done, there
must be only so many ways of hitting the back of the net, but
there are lots and lots of really interesting ways of missing it. The
same isn't true of proper soccer, of course, where goalless draws
are just about on a par with living death, and *Match of the Day*
and so on give them around as much air time.

Law Twenty-two
*All soccer played on the other side of any stretch of water
wider than the Bristol Channel is Subsoccer.*

I finally found, during a trip to America, just how dramatically
false are the ideas that gave us the goal-glut fallacy. It involved
my friend Phil, who inexplicably left the country soon after that
sex-and-drama fiasco in Regent's Park and went to live quietly
in New Jersey. For some reason, he kept his new address secret,
but Nervous Nelson and I eventually ferreted it out and
promptly visited him. Anyway, by then he had wormed his way
into a side that was pushing hard for the local championship,
with just a few games to go and every chance of winning the
League. It wasn't quite New York Cosmos, of course, but even
so, Nervous Nelson and myself weren't exactly prepared for the
monumental dreadfulness of the match we went to watch.

It took place in Brooklyn, I think, or it might have been the
Bronx, on a sandstrip surrounded by dozens of Little League
baseball battles. It was a Sunday morning, but the enlightened
licensing laws in the States meant that we drank so much on the
way that we accidentally arrived early, in time to see the end of
the previous game. (The USA may be a largish country, but it

seems it can only accommodate about eight soccer pitches, shared between around eight thousand teams.) It was pretty awful stuff. One side were fielding only seven men and we shook our heads, sympathised, and got stuck into our six-packs.

'You see this bunch with seven,' growled Phil.

We did.

'They're the reserve side of the Bronx Pinksox (or whoever).'

'Our firsts play their firsts next. Not too hot, are they?'

They weren't, as they were thirteen down, but then they were, as the temperature was pretty nearly tropical. We shook our heads again and gazed philosophically into our Budweisers while Phil ambled off to change. At last the final whistle went and the Pinksox crawled to the dressing-room. Phil's team, the Brooklyn Bodgers (or whatever) then trotted onto the field and waited to start. Two six-packs later they were still waiting. There was much to-ing and fro-ing between the changing-rooms and the pitch and finally, astonishingly, the seven weary Pink-soxers trailed back out. Phil walked across to us.

'You will not believe this,' he told us, 'but the Pinksox first team folded up last night. The League say their reserves have to take over their fixtures, too. We're playing them now.'

'But Phil,' I said, 'they have just played!'

'This is true,' he said, glaring at me.

'But Phil,' said Nelson, 'there are only seven of them.'

'That is also true,' he said, glaring at him.

We all turned and stared at the pathetic wrecks wilting on the other side of the halfway line. I looked at Nelson. Nelson looked at me. We both looked at Phil. It was a far, far better thing we did then than we had ever done before.

'Phil,' I said, 'Phil, we shall play for them.'

He gazed hard at us, and I think there may have been the hint of a tear in his eye (although it might have been the Budweiser).

'Good men,' he said. It was the most emotional speech I have ever heard him make. Phil, as you may have guessed, is not given to deep sentiment. Still, we did feel terribly noble about volunteering, even if I can never remember seeing Nelson quite so Nervous. Back in England, of course, people would have said we were insane, and we would have agreed, but here it was different. We were, we felt, flying the flag. And what about the poor Pinksox themselves, doomed to an epic, all-time devastation? We simply could not stand by and see it done.

A FAR FAR BIGGER FARCE

As it happened, we did. The Pinksox were pitifully grateful for our help, especially when they found we came from Britain where they knew proper soccer sometimes went on. The Bodgers' boss, however, would have none of it. This was, at this point in time, a most important win-big situation, he explained. No way would he give the go-ahead to hand them a couple of crack limey superstars on a plate. We felt that Phil found this unnecessarily amusing.

'Superstars!' he cried. 'Have you seen how these two characters play! Have you seen how much they've drunk!'

The subcoach was adamant. If the Brooklyn Bodgers ran up, say, thirty, he told us, his eyes gleaming, their goal difference would leave their rivals, the New York Hankies, nowhere. In the end Nelson and I gave it up, secretly vastly relieved, and sloped back to the booze.

What followed was without doubt the most one-sided game since the dawn of history. Pinksox held out courageously until the second minute, and then collapsed. The goals just flowed in. After a quarter of an hour it was ten-nil and treble figures seemed a very real possibility. Relaxed by the mixture of sun and Bud, Nelson and I began to enter more seriously into the spirit of things. We took to invading the pitch every time Phil's lot scored, to do little dances of delight. We sent up lunatic chants like 'We want nineteen!' or clenched our fists and shouted, 'Forget those twenty-three! It's still nil-nil!' In the end the sub-coach came striding over to speak to us.

'Say, you guys,' he smiled – he was a nice man, if obsessed by success. 'Say, would you mind toning it down a little? You're kinda turning this into a farce.'

We collapsed. When the hysterics were over, we walked round and round the ground, offering beer to exhausted Pinksox people. To his credit, Phil joined us after a while; he was also the only man on his side who refused to score – even the goalkeeper knocked one in on an overlap. Phil left us just once before the end, and then created total panic by kicking one of the opposition, laying him out on the edge of the penalty box. Reduced to six, everybody realised, the Pinksox couldn't legally continue, and the subref would have no choice but to abandon the match. The entire Bodgers team – except Phil who tactfully withdrew – crowded round the injured man, desperate to help. I have never seen anything quite like it.

At last the poor player was propped up against his own goal-post, and the forty-seventh eventually went in off his shin. (An owl goal in a forty-seven-nil defeat! Even Nervous Nelson was impressed!) There were still twenty minutes to play, but the subref blew his whistle.

'How about it, fellas?' he said. 'I guess we've had about enough of this. Whaddaya say?'

Everyone looked across at the subcoach.

'What is it now?' he called out cheerfully. 'Forty-seven? Yeah, okay, that'll do. Let's call it quits!'

FAR CORNERS

To be fair, subplayers and, indeed, quite normal people who stumble across any sort of game that's going on abroad, do seem to end up knee-deep in absurdity. I couldn't really say why this is, since we all know that there's a lot of very good football played overseas. It's just that it never seems to involve us. It's far simpler to be prepared by accepting Law Twenty-two – 'All soccer played on the other side of any stretch of water wider than the Bristol Channel is Subsoccer' – and expect the worst.

Not to say that subteams aren't successful when they travel, to the Continent, for example. For one thing, being subteams, they are quite immune to ploys such as the one practised by the French, which involves encouraging visiting clubs to eat and drink huge quantities in pre-match banquets. This never affects the British subside, who are quite happy with such a mode of preparation, but it very often upsets the French players themselves, kept both hungry and sober. Bitterly angry at missing out on all the fun, they spend the game shrugging their shoulders, muttering darkly about *Monsieur le President*, and forgetting to tackle.

Even when they don't manage to take advantage of all this, British subclubs usually return at least *looking* successful. Whenever any of these European teams organise the mini-tournaments to which they so kindly invite us, they always put up incredibly ornate trophies for everyone to play for. You are very unlucky if you don't get a good one simply for turning up. This means you can come back carrying all kinds of silverware, which quite impresses ordinary holidaymakers who don't realise the truth.

I remember one stupendous tour of Dieppe when we walked off with an enormous object, a sort of cross between a vase and a silver saucepan. There were thirteen of us on the trip – twelve players and a cardboard cut-out called Achille who'd done well at left back – and I'm sure the whole lot of us could have fitted quite comfortably inside. On the way home, in fact, we couldn't work out whether to take the cup onto the ferry or to pop the ferry inside the cup. As someone pointed out, however, we were

better off on the boat; the trophy was very nice, but it didn't
have an all-night bar.

To be honest, not every side that goes on these tours does
quite so well. We have all heard stories of North London den-
tists, for instance, who turn up in Germany to find the locals
expecting Tottenham Hotspur, and then lose twenty-six-nil to
Bayern Munich. Or terrible reports of clubs called, say, Solihull
Nomads, who aren't quite Wolverhampton Wanderers but go
to Italy and then watch Roma whack thirty-five into their
net. (Come to think of it, that might have been Wolves after
all.)

The misunderstandings tend to be tiny but at the same time
tremendous: instead of a team from *the* English First Division
you end up with a side from *an* English First Division – from the
First Division in Potters Bar, perhaps. At times like these the
lines about corners of foreign fields come to mind; or at least
they would do, except that the poor subteams are pinned in their
own penalty box for the whole ninety minutes and never
actually see the corners at all.

GOING SOLO

In some ways subsoccermen can have even more fun when they
go abroad alone, or at least without their usual subteam. It's
then possible really to enjoy yourself by either looking at or
playing in matches even more awful than the kind you know so
well at home.

I shall never forget one débacle I witnessed in Ibiza, between
the San Antonio town side and another from some nearby salt
mines. At least, I think they were from the salt mines – my Spa-
nish is not brilliant. San Antonio won about eight-three, which
was funny enough in itself, but apart from that they had a
unique way of keeping score. Every time the home team got a
goal, somebody fired a cannon. Apparently they did this to let

Every time the home team got a goal, somebody fired a cannon.

the fishermen out in the harbour and the disc jockeys down in the discos know what was going on. Massacres like the one I went to may well have deafened most of the Western Mediterranean – I'm sure people across in Mallorca thought war had broken out on the other island. I couldn't help wondering how we would cope with that sort of system over here. I don't suppose we could cope with it at all, without arranging for those soldiers to be on stand-by, who fire twenty-one gun salutes to the Queen. And would the Royal Horse Artillery really turn out on a wet Sunday morning? Hackney Marshes are hardly Hyde Park, after all.

Mind you, I've seen pitches on the Continent that make the Marshes look quite magnificent. I've even played on one of them. It was out in Northern Greece, on a 'field' that couldn't manage one single blade of grass but was made up entirely of rolled dirt. This naturally made slide tackling fairly unpopular, but when I played on it for my friend's village side, that was exactly what I tried to do. I had to. I had been put at right back and been told to mark – wait for it – a left winger!

It could only happen in Greece, the home of legendary beings, but there he was, and unfortunately he turned out to be pretty good, which meant I tended to kick him. This upset the poor chap a little, and he became even more annoyed when I tried to talk to him. I only knew about five words of the Greek language, and in all the excitement I forgot three of them. All I could say, in the end, was 'Hello' and 'Thank you'. This I repeated every time I flattened him, until he very sensibly gave up and went and stood at left back. My friend told me that the way I played had convinced the other team I was Italian. I have never felt so proud in my life.

Sadly enough, it couldn't last, not even until the final whistle, since for once this never sounded. A quarter of an hour into the second half, I noticed the people on the touchline peering into the distance, shrugging their shoulders, and getting ready to leave. This seemed odd, since it was a pleasant evening with a nice, refreshing breeze, but I soon saw why. Seconds later, the refreshing breeze had become a very fair hurricane, the traditional tornado that whips down through Thessalonica from the mountains of Yugoslavia.

Within minutes this typhoon had smartly picked up most of our dirt track and dropped it neatly into the harbour. We've all watched players leave the pitch, but this must be the only time that anyone has seen the pitch leave the players.

Law Twenty-three
The only sound more meaningless than the noise produced by those watching a Subsoccer match is the noise produced by those playing it.

I must admit I was very sorry that I couldn't understand what the crowd were saying when that match in Thessalonica ended with the field swirling off into the sunset. I'm sure the Greeks – even the Greek subfans – had a word for it. Back home, of course, spectators would be dangerously upset to hear a referee declaring the ground unfit, or indeed, declaring the ground gone, which I suppose is what he did there.

So long as the game goes ahead, however, people watching Subsoccer generally tend to be fairly well-behaved. This may be because there's so much hooliganism out there on the pitch that there's simply no point in starting up any more on the touchline. They're very unlikely to offend people with any of those rather silly chants, either: subfans can't chant at all, mainly because their teams have such strange names. Can you imagine anyone composing a catchy little ditty that could fit in, say, Crouch End Vampires, or Collier Row Motor Gear Reserves? (I promise you these clubs do exist.) The only proper side that gives its supporters the same sort of trouble must be Hamilton Academicals.

In any case, more noise comes from mockery than from admiration, and on bad days this can flow into a steady stream of monotonous abuse. Subplayers usually need to be fairly close to the touchline to catch this, since the watchers, even less healthy than those they watch, don't have the lungs for the long-range insult. This is just as well, as the players themselves aren't too keen on taking a constant verbal battering, and may even leave the pitch to try to stop it.

Still, it can be funny. I remember one Sunday team in Kew I used to go and look at solely because of their one longsuffering supporter. For some reason he took an insane dislike to his side's inoffensive right winger, a mild-mannered little man called Quentin. Every game he would give a blow-by-blow report on his all-round awfulness.

'Don't give it to ... Oh, God! Oh no ... He's ... He's given it to Quentin! Quentin's got it! Quentin's got it! Quentin's awful! Quentin's useless ... He's ... Oh, God! Look at him! He's not going to ... He is! He is ... Don't! Don't, Quentin, you moron! Don't! Oh no! Look ... He's ... He's going to lose it! He is! He's going to lose it! He's going to ... There! He's lost it! Quentin's lost it! Quentin! Quentin!'

THE LEFT WING KICK-OFF
Since the Quentin Critic and others like him spend so much of the match helpless with despair and/or laughter, subplayers don't often need to worry about less verbal forms of violence. I can, however, think of one exception.

It happened when my Sunday side were going through a poor run in front of goal – we hadn't scored for three months. We were so bad, in fact, that we decided we simply had to make the most of the only DBS we were always sure to get – the kick-off. We let in so many, you see, that we were certain to end up with lots in every game. Eventually we felt we'd come up with a winner.

It was based, fittingly enough, on the rugby model. Most of the team would line up along the left of the halfway line, the ball would be knocked back to somebody standing where right half once used to stand, and he would then belt it high upfield towards the left-hand corner of the penalty box, with our lot charging after it. Every now and then, we thought, the ball and the charge would arrive at roughly the same time, and anything could happen, even a goal. We called the move the Left Wing Kick-Off, with the up-and-under the Strato Ball, since it spent such a long time up in the stratosphere. The first time we used it, we scored.

Well, almost. In fact we scrambled a corner, which went in off the right back's elbow. This meant that the Left Wing Kick-Off was voted a huge success, and we agreed to use it for the rest of the season. As it happened, there was only one game left in the season, but that turned out to be against a team that had to beat us to win the League. And that was where the subfans, and the trouble, came in.

The entire gang of players, officials and supporters of the side that stood to win the title if we didn't lose the match, came along to watch, convinced we were going to clinch the championship for them. This worried us, but at least we made a good start by winning the toss and setting up the Strato. And then we realised we had nobody to play it.

It was all our keeper's fault. He had a 'cousin' staying at his flat and had promised, he told us, to show her the sights. Whether that involved actually leaving his flat we didn't know, but it did leave me standing in goal. Since I was the man who

kicked in the Left Wing Kick-Off, that presented a problem; or
at least it would have done, but I decided I'd better go and kick it
anyway.

I took up my usual spot, leaving the goal empty behind me,
while most of the others lined up for the forward rush. The
opposing team thought we were crazy, and so did the referee. He
blew for the start, and immediately blew again, to stop things.

'Look here,' he said, 'are you quite sure this sort of thing is
legal?'

'Definitely,' said our captain. 'The ref let us do it last week,
and he was a Richmond councillor.' This wasn't strictly true,
but it obviously impressed our man, and we set ourselves up all
over again.

I was beginning to have second thoughts by now, but the
whistle went and the ball was played back towards me. I say
'played', but in fact it was more – sort of 'scuffed'. It was probably the very worst pass I have ever had in my life, bobbling at
me so slowly that I was sure it was about to start going backwards; however, I moved to meet it as our collective left wing
thundered into their box. Just as I swung into the Strato Kick, it
took one last super-bobble and hopped neatly over my foot. The
other lot's whippet winger, covering the twenty yards between
us in about nought-point-one seconds, nipped past me to run the
ball into the deserted net while I fell to the ground, unable to
watch.

Our flying wedge had stopped racing towards the other end
by now, and was staring hopefully into the sky, waiting for the
ball that would never come. In the end, four of them had to be
led back to the halfway line by the sympathetic subref, who later
told us he had timed the goal at three and a quarter seconds. We
did not use the Left Wing Kick-Off again.

Watching all this, of course, were approximately thirty men
expecting to see us lay down our lives for their glory. Needless to

say, they were not exactly overjoyed with us. And they were even less overjoyed with me than they were with everyone else. All thirty lumbered round to stand behind my goal, where one or two suggested I ought to do a little better. I agreed. No, but really, they said. I agreed again. With them to encourage me, I then played the game of my life, saving everything in sight and hoping that might save my skin. In the end we went two down to an unstoppable own goal that flew in off our centre half's nose, which my fan club didn't like at all.

'He didn't mean it,' I told them. 'Honestly.'

None of them said anything, although a couple spat. Finally their chief spokesthug, a thorough-going gorilla about six foot tall and seven foot wide, came and thrust his face at me.

'You ——— You ——— ——— ———. You and your ——— team are ——— ———,' he informed me. 'We're not wasting a ——— morning watching you ———. We're off to the pub down the road. Just make sure you're not there. Ever. Now ———.'

With that, they went away, although from what the spokesthug said I thought I should have gone instead. A couple of weeks later we heard that their club had resigned from the League in disgust, so perhaps it wasn't quite such a bad day's work after all.

A LOSING STREAK

That bunch broke one of the unwritten laws of subspectating, I suppose, by persuading me to play a little better than I thought I could. I really can't remember anyone else who stopped a side of mine losing by more than we should have. But I doubt if I shall ever forget one subfan who very kindly explained why we were losing at all.

To be fair, we did have a pretty good idea anyway; it was because we were one short. What we didn't know was why we were one short. It was a particularly bad game in which to be one short, a students' grudge match between King's and University College, a few miles outside London. These affairs make the average civil war look very tame indeed, and UC, realising they had one too many for us to kick, very sensibly began to knock us silly. We were cursing our missing man – a tough, no-frills Geordie – when a girl turned up to tell us that he was in gaol.

Now this was very strange because, a) we couldn't believe that anyone had built a gaol that could hold him, and b) we couldn't believe a girl had come along to tell us about it. Usually, you see, there are even fewer spectators at student Subsoccer matches than at any others, not even the proverbial one man and his dog. The lack of dogs never really worries substudents, nor does the lack of men, but the lack of ladies does. For some strange reason, girls seem fatally attracted to university rugby games, and flock to them in droves. Only those who fail auditions as rugby club groupies ever mooch along to watch soccer, and even then they can be seen gazing longingly at the scrums and line-outs going on in the distance. All of which made the sudden appearance of this subfemale even more startling.

'The pigs have snatched Dave,' she announced dramatically. (She was rather a radical.)

Play stopped completely.

'Yeah, the pigs,' she went on. (She was a rather repetitive radical.) 'All he did was do a streak in Trafalgar Square.'

Needless to say, UC, who had looked a little worried for a minute, treated us with even more contempt after that and gave us a truly terrible tanning. Dave himself may now be very keen to forget the incident – these days he is a respectable insurance broker – but at the time he seemed to enjoy it. There was even a picture of him in *The Sun*, a passing pigeon conveniently covering the parts other papers never reach. When the case finally came to court, and the magistrate asked if he really thought people were at all interested in what he'd displayed, he endeared himself to the public gallery (if not to the magistrate) by answering, 'Yes.' We more or less forgave Dave in the end, but nobody I know has ever bought one of his insurance policies.

A RUNNING COMMENTARY

I don't remember exactly what we said out there on the pitch when that girl brought the news about Dave, but I'm sure it wasn't anything very amusing. At other times, subplayers really can be terribly funny, usually when they're trying to be terribly serious.

This often happens when they're begging to be given the ball. I actually heard someone shout 'Russell – square!' once, and I can think of a whole list of calls which seemed every bit as comical. I've stood and smiled at 'Round the back, Jack! Flick it on, Ron! On my head, Fred! Pass to us, Gus! Go for goal, Noel! Give 'em hell, Tel! Down the wing, er – Thing!' and, my own favourite, 'On the edge, Reg!'

Still, even this can't compare with the monologue in motion I listened to in another Sunday game. It was meant to be a desperate relegation struggle – most Sunday games are desperate relegation struggles – but as it turned out, we approached this one in a rather relaxed manner. (We were all drunk.)

We were playing somewhere in Twickenham, and in the second half Mike, our part-time centre forward and full-time eccentric, got hold of the ball just outside our penalty box, put his foot on it, and held up his hand.

'Right, you lot,' he announced. 'This is it. This is the first pass I've had for forty minutes, and I'm going to make the most of it. I'm going to score.'

He then put his head down and ran, jinking, weaving – and babbling.

'I'm on my way! I'm on my way!' he yelled. 'I've beaten one man! I've beaten two!' He had. 'I'm over the halfway line! I've

'I've beaten one man! I've beaten two! I'm over the halfway
line...'

slipped it past the full back! I've slipped it past the full back and I'm still going!' He was. 'I'm going well! The centre half's coming across to cover! What do I do now?'

'Sure, cut inside, Mike!' bawled Gus, his co-eccentric.

'Right! I will! I'll cut inside!' shouted the flying forward. 'I've ... I've cut inside! I'm going into the box! I'm going in! Here I go! I'm in the box! Here comes the sweeper! He's going to kick me! He's ... He's kicked me! He's kicked me, but I'm still going! And here's the keeper! Here he is! I'll push it past him! I will! I have! I've pushed it past him! I've pushed it past him and I've scored! I've scored! I've scored! What a goal!'

He turned away in triumph, tried a celebration somersault, twisted his ankle, and had to be helped off, still jabbering. ('I'm going off! I've twisted my ankle and I'm going off!') Strangely enough, the other team were not amused.

'For God's sake, he told you what he was going to do,' grumbled their captain. 'Why didn't you stop him!'

CATCH A FALLING BAR

Mike's running commentary, of course, was a neat reminder of Law Twenty-three – 'The only sound more meaningless than the noise produced by those watching a Subsoccer match is the noise produced by those playing it.' I can't actually say I've ever heard anything more bizarre in the way of odd broadcasts, but I suppose the closest thing to it came years ago in a game between two Boys' Brigade sides.

I was sneakily turning out for one of them (I was really a Cub) and wishing I hadn't, since we were taking an awful pasting. This was mostly because of our goalkeeper, whose style was, to say the least, a little unusual. Whenever the other lot got anywhere near his area he would hide his head in his hands and start gibbering.

'Oh no! Here it comes again! Oh no! It's going to do it again! I know it is! Oh no! Oh no!'

He would then stand there, eyes tightly closed, until the ball bounced gently past him for yet another goal. Then he cheered up a little.

'Has it gone in? Has it? It has? It's a goal? Really? A goal? Oh good!'

Being a new member of the side, this puzzled me a little, until the left back explained. Apparently the keeper had been rather upset a couple of weeks before when a shot hit the bar, which promptly dropped on his head, knocking him scatty.

'And he's afraid it might happen again, you see,' said the other lad. 'Sad, isn't it? Hasn't been the same player since.'

I wondered why they put up with him.

'We're just hoping he'll grow out of it,' I was told. 'And, besides, his mother washes the kit.'

Law Twenty-four
There are lies, damned lies, and Subsoccer reports.

Subsoccermen love to see all these episodes written up in the local papers. It's only when they actually read about the things that happen in their submatches that some of them can be convinced that they've happened at all. It also helps them to feel, just for a while, a tiny part of proper soccer. Unfortunately, the reports which appear are not produced by upright, incorruptible, objective and sober journalists, but by the subplayers themselves.

Given the basic megalomania of everyone who's ever miskicked a ball in anger, this is quite fatal. Accounts of submatches often make interesting reading, but are unfortunately never, ever true, because Law Twenty-four is strictly adhered to at all times. This observance can be dangerous. I heard of one hopeless case who somehow wormed his way into a successful side up in

Blackpool that ran up cricket scores on a fairly regular basis, while he himself hardly ever scored at all. In one season in which he couldn't notch even one goal (although he did manage to miss seven penalties) the local Football Green had him down for at least a hat-trick every week. You can guess who did the writing.

Nemesis finally arrived when, in a cup quarter final, the club had to take on a fairly tough team made up of Fleetwood trawlermen. They'd obviously done their homework on Lancashire's answer to Roy of the Rovers, and kicked him enthusiastically for the full ninety minutes. He tried to tell the fishermen, in between assaults, that stories of his deadly striking had been ever so slightly exaggerated. Looking at the way he played, they said, they thought he was probably right, but they kept on kicking him all the same, just in case.

As I say, however, he was by no means unique. None of these imaginative articles ever carries a by-line, but it's by no means difficult to work out who's written what. Read, for instance, that 'Red Star Rotherhithe were beaten 27–2, but Boyle had a superb game in goal', and it's clear that Mr Boyle was the man who picked up the pen. On the other hand, 'Partisan Plaistow went down 9–0, but Blatter often came close to pulling a couple back' is plainly a contribution from Mr Blatter.

NELSON AND THE NAÏVE

I believe the only exception to this dishonesty comes in the reports written by my friend, Nervous Nelson, who carefully keeps his own name out of print. His particular trademark is one of tone, which he calls the Naïve Style, a kind of colossal simplicity that makes him feel like Halsted's answer to Ernest Hemingway – although many put him rather closer to Enid Blyton. His accounts go something like this:

'We went to ground. We kicked off. They scored. We did not. At half time we had some tea. The tea was very nice. The second half took place. They scored again. It rained. We lost. What is the point?'

And so on. Sometimes I feel that Nelson's Naïve Style is touched by a sort of daft genius. So simple, and yet so stupid.

WANGLES AND JANGLES

At least there aren't too many factual errors in Nelson's own reports, mainly because there aren't too many facts. Elsewhere, it's quite impossible to be sure whether you can believe even the most basic details. For example, readers can never be completely certain about the actual result. Subteams who have taken quite terrible batterings sometimes try to brazen away their embarrassment by simply lying to the local paper, and every now and then they succeed. It can be very strange if this tactic begins to work on a regular basis, and I remember one side which seemed to win every single week but somehow ended the season with no points at all.

From time to time even the authorities themselves join in the cover-up – not, admittedly, to reverse a result, but at least to wangle it in such a way that it seems more respectable. No subleague likes to see its clubs constantly going down to gigantic defeats, since it makes the whole thing look rather silly, and the odd spot of sympathetic censoring isn't altogether unknown. Proper soccer scores are so much more impressive, after all; I can think of one team that, twice within a few days, lost by a clear twenty goals, only to read they had gone down by a very reasonable 2–0 each time. Nobody ever really missed the odd nought, I suppose.

Even if you decide to accept any of this, it can be a little difficult to come to terms with the way it's all presented. I knew a club secretary who always managed to twist his match reports into a sort of secret poetry, which jingled and jangled all over the weekly sports editions for several months. His little offerings would include passages along these lines:

'But then, with half an hour to go they made it one apiece.
Corcoran crossed it hard and low and in it went from Preece.
The home side now were well on top – they looked a little fitter.
The keeper made a brilliant stop and Redfern missed a sitter.
They hit the post and then we knew the winner had to come.
Edwards picked up number two with a volley off his knee...'

And so it went on, as if someone had signed William Words-
worth to cover soccer for *The Sun*.

A SEND-UP TOO MANY

I must admit that for many years I saw very little wrong with
most of this. We are, after all, dealing with the subgame and, as I
so often stress, fantasy is fundamental. I was a little surprised to
find that one newspaper I worked for had taken things a stage
further, allowing a Football League club's press officer to write
rather sympathetic reports on his own team. Even then, I still felt
the traditional do-it-yourself journalism seemed safe enough at
lower levels: it took the sheer lunacy of one especially insane
subclub to persuade me that even this had to be very positively
vetted.

The guilty men were a notoriously rebellious Sunday side in
West London, a team that had once been very good indeed,
about ten years before, but had been sliding steadily into me-
diocrity ever since. As they became worse, they began to take
revenge on the game that had betrayed them by sending up the
whole silly business.

It wasn't just the reports they wrote for the unsuspecting local
paper, although these were bad enough. They appeared bursting
with names so improbable that even subplayers – who, as I've
said, tend to be an odd-sounding bunch – shook their heads and
wondered. Week after week we read about people called Bonk,

Oomph, Garp, Sausage, Stump, Cistern, Tuba, Plectrum and even, once, Aardvaark.

Amazingly, they got away with all that, possibly because the sports editor simply piled everything from his in-tray into his columns in a bout of Monday morning lethargy. Strangely enough, what finished them were the team lists they started to send in for the next weekend. These ran something like this:

'Northside United (meet Sunday, 9.30 am, Wormwood Scrubs). R. Biggs, R. Kray, R. Kray, D. Crippin, D. Nielsen, B. Edwards, D. Turpin, A. Capone, N. Kelly, R. Hood, J.T. Ripper, B. Strangler.'

Or, 'Northside United (meet Sunday, 9.45 am, Sunbury Conservative Club). E. Heath, A. Eden, S. Baldwin, J. Prior, H. Macmillan, B. Disraeli, N. Tebbitt, D. Bonar-Law, A. Douglas-Home, N. Chamberlain, W.S. Churchill. Sub: M. Thatcher.'

Still they weren't caught out, even when they claimed they were meeting outside the Crossroads Motel with a back-four that read 'A. Turtle, M. Richardson, D. Hunter, and B. Enny.' The sports editor's Monday morning lethargy obviously began some time on the Friday before. The side that finally broke the camel's back, as it were, were meant to rendezvous outside the Shepperton Showbiz Club, with F. Sinatra picked to play up front. At this the poor journalist exploded into a sort of apopleptic fit.

'Are they trying to make me look a fool?' he yelled. 'Him turning out up front for Northside! Everybody knows he plays midfield for Athletico Acton!'

Law Twenty-five
In any given game of Subsoccer, the majority of those on the pitch should not be there, even when they should be.

To be fair, even relatively normal subclubs face very definite problems when it comes to team lists. For a manager to publish the real names of the men who usually play for his side, for instance, would certainly result in heavy fines, since virtually none of them will be signed on. Keen-eyed league secretaries, who spend whole years of their lives poring over match cards, put in just as long reading through match reports. It's all part of their constant quest for the pleasure of 'spotting the ringer', and they hardly ever fail.

There is absolutely no need for this, in fact. Emergency late replacements are something else again, but the point is that even regular subplayers turn out year after year for the same club without ever signing the form that would make honest men of them all. So just why don't they make it legal? Nobody knows. Most submen can manage to write their own names, so long as they've given enough time, so that can't be the reason. In the end it's probably down to that subconscious anarchy, the refusal to accept that anything as chaotic as Subsoccer can be subject to any rules or regulations at all. And in any case, does it really matter? As Shakespeare almost said, a rogue by any other name...

THE RINGER REVEALED

Since we do have all those irritating laws about eligibility, the fact is that A. Rogue, or whoever, needs to be signed on to satisfy the bewildered bureaucrats who fret over the local subgame. Or rather, he needs to pretend to be signed on.

It's for this reason that so many subplayers can be seen standing in dressing-room corners before matches, muttering to themselves. They are not praying, even though they probably should be, but trying to memorise who they're meant to be. Once they're on the pitch, of course, they immediately forget, which can be difficult if team-mates insist on calling them by their assumed names.

This is one reason for so many perfectly sensible calls being ignored during the game (another is creeping deafness). The worst moments come when one of these counterfeits gets himself booked. Hours can drag by as he tries to remember his temporary identity while the subref stands patiently by, pencil in hand. It isn't long before the other side start to realise what's going on. They then gather round, dancing little jigs of delight, pointing and jeering.

'He's a ringer! He's a ringer!' they cry.

At last the poor fraud will blurt out anything that pops into his baffled brain. 'M. Mouse', I've heard people say, or 'R. Reagan', and even, once, 'P. Charles', which would have worked if the man could have decided what the 'P' stood for. Most tragic of all, however, are those who can't make even this pathetic effort.

'Name!' demands the subref. 'Give me your name!' And after a while, they break down completely.

'I don't know!' they gibber. 'I don't know!'

ANONYMOUS, NEWCASTLE

Sometimes subplayers do have very good cause to remain anonymous, or at least incognito. I have a friend from the North-East who came across one individual rather anxious to escape any kind of publicity during a game up in Newcastle.

My friend was playing in midfield, and was surprised to see he would be marking a lad he'd known in school, the one-time class tough-guy he hadn't met for well over five years. Anyway, they had a fine old time, chasing one another up and down the pitch and taking it in turns to hack at each other's shins. To celebrate their reunion, they even stood back every so often to smile at misplaced wall passes (there are no one-twos in Subsoccer; only ones), and generally had a fine old time.

Unfortunately, with all this going on, they simply couldn't fit

'I was inside,' he said quietly. 'Still am, officially. Escaped last night . . .'

in any sort of chat until they limped off the pitch together at the end of the match.

'Howay, Matt (or something),' gasped my friend. 'Haven't seen you for ages, man.'

'Aye,' answered Matt.

'Hey, heard a lot about you, though,' said my friend. 'Heard you were inside. Attempted manslaughter, or something.'

Matt looked quickly around him, and moved closer.

'I was,' he said quietly. 'Still am, officially. Escaped last night. So you still haven't seen me. Have you.'

It was not a question. My friend gulped, shook his head, and slunk away, too scared even to stop for a shower. It was the only time in his life, he told me later, that he almost had his leg broken on a football field by a man who wasn't even there.

But by being there and by being both somewhere else and someone else at the same time, the Mysterious Matt did underline the subsport's twenty-fifth and final law: 'In any given game of Subsoccer, the majority of those on the pitch should not be there, even when they should be.'

Need I say more?

Epilogue

ON FIRST LOOKING INTO KING'S SUBSOCCER

A subgame sonnet, with apologies to
John Keats, John Charles, John Motson, etc.

Much have I travelled in the realms of mud,
And many awful fields and pitches seen;
Round many one-way systems have I been
Which stopped me going where I thought I should.
They said I never would be any good
At soccer, and it's true my times were lean,
But now I play with temperament serene
Since I read King write each can if he could.
Then felt I like the man between the sticks
When a soggy football drops into his lap.
Or like stout forwards, when with feeble kicks
They score Weetabix goals, and the team clap,
Then rub their eyes as if their sight plays tricks,
Silent upon a swamp at Watford Gap.

                                        Anon.

163

The Laws of Subsoccer

Law One: Subsoccer is likely to occur at any time under any given set of conditions, but just as likely not to.

Law Two: There are no laws in Subsoccer, not even this one, and if there are they are not very often applied anyway.

Law Three: Add half-and-hour to the time agreed for any meeting before the game, but one hour if there is a decent pub in the area or a big race on television.

Law Four: No Subsoccer motorist is capable of following a given car over a distance greater than twenty-five yards under any circumstances whatever.

Law Five: No matter how big they seem, all Subsoccer dressing-rooms are too small.

Law Six: No pre-match warm-up ever ends before the players are freezing cold.

Law Seven: The ability to talk about the game in the bar will be in inverse proportion to the ability to play the game on the pitch.

Law Eight: Goalkeepers go away, but goalkicks don't.

Law Nine: Nothing ever reaches the far post.

Law Ten: Each and every defensive wall has a hole in the middle, and so has each and every goalkeeper.

Law Eleven: The game on the next pitch is always better than yours, even when it is worse.

Law Twelve: Most Subsoccer teams constantly start one short, and so do many players.

Law Thirteen: Everything and everyone enjoys a visit to a Subsoccer ground, except, of course, those who have anything at all to do with the match.

Law Fourteen: Anything that might not fit, will not fit.

Law Fifteen: The ability of any subteam stands in inverse proportion to the brilliance of its colours and the sophistication of its name.

Law Sixteen: Referees should be seen and not heard, except when they are not even seen at all.

Law Seventeen: Each and every club linesman except Sid is so bent that it would be impossible to hang his picture straight on the wall.

Law Eighteen: Foul play is quite acceptable, but foul language is a capital offence.

Law Nineteen: The only good referee is a bad referee.

Law Twenty: All submatches are refereed by everyone on the pitch with the exception of the referee.

Law Twenty-one: Not everyone likes watching soccer, but anybody watching Subsoccer likes it even less than anyone else.

Law Twenty-two: All soccer played on the other side of any stretch of water wider than the Bristol Channel is Subsoccer.

Law Twenty-three: The only sound more meaningless than the noise produced by those watching a Subsoccer match is the noise produced by those playing in it.

Law Twenty-four: There are lies, damned lies, and Subsoccer reports.

Law Twenty-five: In any given game of Subsoccer, the majority of those on the pitch should not be there, even when they should be.